Revisiting
The Duty to Consult
Aboriginal Peoples

Revisiting
The Duty to Consult
Aboriginal Peoples

Dwight G. Newman

PURICH
PUBLISHING
LIMITED
SASKATOON, SK. CANADA

Purich Publishing Ltd.
Box 23032, Market Mall Post Office, Saskatoon, SK, Canada, S7J 5H3
Phone: (306) 373-5311 Fax: (306) 373-5315 Email: purich@sasktel.net
www.purichpublishing.com

Library and Archives Canada Cataloguing in Publication

Newman, Dwight
[Duty to consult]
    Revisiting the duty to consult Aboriginal peoples / Dwight G. Newman. — Revised edition.

Revision of: The duty to consult : new relationships with Aboriginal peoples / Dwight G. Newman.
Includes bibliographical references and index.
ISBN 978-1-895830-81-1 (pbk.)

    1. Native peoples — Legal status, laws, etc. — Canada. 2. Native peoples — Canada — Government relations. 3. Native peoples — Canada — Claims. 4. Constitutional law — Canada — Cases. I. Title. II. Title: Duty to consult Aboriginal peoples.

KE7709.N49 2014   342.7108'72   C2014-902630-7
KF8205.N49 2014

Edited, designed, and typeset by Donald Ward.
Cover design by D.J. Olson, Olson Information Design.
Index by Ursula Acton.
Cover image: iStock.

Purich Publishing gratefully acknowledges the assistance of the Government of Canada through the Canada Book Fund, and the Creative Industry Growth and Sustainability Program made possible through funding provided to the Saskatchewan Arts Board by the Government of Saskatchewan through the Ministry of Parks, Culture and Sport for its publishing program.

Printed on 100 per cent post-consumer, recycled, ancient-forest-friendly paper.

Contents

Acknowledgements

THIS BOOK IS A SUBSTANTIALLY REVISED AND EXPANDED VERSION of *The Duty to Consult: New Relationships with Aboriginal Peoples*, which was originally published by Purich Publishing in 2009. Developments since 2009, of course, as well as the opportunity to reflect further on the duty to consult, have made it both imperative and possible to come back to the project in new ways. I appreciate the belief of Karen Bolstad and Don Purich at Purich Publishing in this project for both that first edition and for this substantially revised book. Their enthusiasm and patience in the face of a longer writing process than anticipated — both times — have made it possible to prepare a book that I hope will continue to make a contribution. I am honoured to have had both editions of this book appear as part of their distinguished line of books on Aboriginal, legal, and western Canadian issues.

Donald Ward, who has edited both editions, has done much to help make the book accessible to a wider audience, so that the book can be read not only by lawyers but by non-lawyers as well. Remaining legalese has been despite efforts on his part to help make it more accessible. I also thank Ursula Acton for her skilled indexing of the book.

I appreciate the work of various research assistants who have worked with me on duty to consult issues, with those doing the most in relation to this book including Danielle Schweitzer, Nicole Cargill, and Laura Forseille, although I would be remiss if I did not also thank Michelle Biddulph, Lorelle Binnion, Lorne Fagnan, Scott Hitchings, and Amy Jo Scherman. I am also grateful for interactions with graduate students working on related topics, especially Jamie Dickson.

I am grateful for Social Sciences and Humanities Research Council (SSHRC) funding that has helped with research on both editions, and I am also grateful for support from the Canada Research Chairs program in later years.

I have presented on or engaged in discussions about the duty to consult in numerous contexts over recent years, ranging from Canadian Bar Association (CBA) events and the National Judicial Institute to workshops in Aboriginal communities and at Aboriginal mining forums, from Crown corporation workshops to world mining conferences, and from legal theory workshops at other law schools to Arctic law meetings. It is not possible to thank all whose comments and queries have been of use but, at the risk of leaving out others who have been equally helpful, I do express my gratitude to individuals who include but are not limited to Natasha Affolder, Ravina Bains, Nigel Bankes, John Borrows, Marie-Ann Bowden, Naomi Carriere, Ken Coates, Paul Chartrand, Eric Cline, Wesley Cragg, Michelle Delorme, Chris Donald, Gordon Dupre, Mark Ebert, Sonia Eggerman, Patricia Farnese, Tom Flanagan, George Foster, Sari Graben, Sébastien Grammond, Robin Hansen, Heather Heavin, Felix Hoehn, Leah Howie, Celeste Hutchinson, James (Sa'ke'j) Youngblood Henderson, Courtney Kirk, Patrick Macklem, Preston Manning, Mitch McAdam, Dan McGill, Tom McKenzie, Kent McNeil, Robert Miller, David Milward, Liam Mooney, Ronalda Murphy, Val Napoleon, Bram Noble, Rob Norris, Ibironke Odumosu-Ayanu, Greg Poelzer, Marilyn Poitras, Janna Promislow, Brian Slattery, David Schneiderman, Marjorie Simington, Chuck Strahl, David Watson, John Whyte, and Danielle Yeager.

In the interests of full disclosure, I should state also that I have, in a small number of instances, provided objective legal opinions to government agencies on means of complying appropriately with the duty to consult. Those opportunities, like other engagement with pertinent stakeholders and communities, have been intellectually enriching in better understanding some of the on-the-ground consequences of the duty to consult.

The ultimate book product, of course, reflects my own scholarly engagement with the duty to consult doctrine and my own thinking on this topic. I hope it will contribute to ongoing conversations in the years ahead.

Dwight G. Newman
Saskatoon
April 2014

Preface to the Revised Edition

RECENT ABORIGINAL CASE LAW IN CANADA has been largely concerned with elaborating the implications of the Aboriginal rights provision in s. 35 of the *Constitution Act, 1982*.[1] Over the past ten years, this body of law has become increasingly dominated by the case law of a new doctrine: the duty to consult. This duty has enormous legal and policy implications and is of major public interest. Some skeptical voices have argued along the way that the duty to consult is not meaningful because it does not grant Aboriginal communities a veto over development,[2] but the elaboration of the duty to consult doctrine has had major impacts in policy contexts and on approaches to decision-making that may affect Aboriginal communities. This book will partly elaborate on some of these impacts.

The first edition of this book, published in 2009, appeared five years after the development of the significantly revised duty to consult doctrine. The duties of consultation have been recognized in certain contexts for a longer period — particularly as part of the justification test first set out in *R. v. Sparrow*[3] for infringements of Aboriginal rights protected by s. 35. Recent discussion, however, springs from a trilogy of cases in 2004 and 2005: the *Haida Nation* case,[4] the *Taku River Tlingit First Nation* case,[5] and the *Mikisew Cree First Nation* case.[6] These three cases actually did much to

---

1   *Constitution Act, 1982*, s. 35, being Schedule B to the *Canada Act 1982* (U.K.), 1982, c. 11. This book presumes a basic understanding of s. 35, which states that "existing aboriginal and treaty rights of the aboriginal peoples of Canada are hereby recognized and affirmed." Misunderstandings of s. 35 sometimes plague discussion of the duty to consult.

2   See Gordon Christie, "A Colonial Reading of Recent Jurisprudence: Sparrow, Delgamuukw and Haida Nation" (2005) 23 Windsor Yearbook of Access to Justice 17.

3   *R. v. Sparrow*, [1990] 1 S.C.R. 1075, 70 D.L.R. (4th) 385.

4   *Haida Nation v. British Columbia (Minister of Forests)*, 2004 SCC 73, [2004] 3 S.C.R. 511.

5   *Taku River Tlingit First Nation v. British Columbia (Project Assessment Director)*, 2003 SCC 74, [2004] 3 S.C.R. 550.

6   *Mikisew Cree First Nation v. Canada (Minister of Canadian Heritage)*, 2005

set Aboriginal rights in Canada, and Aboriginal/non-Aboriginal relations, on a fundamentally different course than they were on before.

However, since 2009, there have been many important developments on the duty to consult. Among these developments have been major Supreme Court of Canada decisions in the *Rio Tinto* case,[7] the *Little Salmon* case,[8] the *Moses* case,[9] and the *Behn/Moulton Contracting* case.[10] Both the Supreme Court of Canada and lower courts have grappled with many questions that they had not previously answered, although their very attempts have opened yet new questions. Governments, Aboriginal communities, and industry stakeholders have engaged with the duty to consult in new and probably unexpected ways, developing policy statements or practices that build upon the duty to consult but often use it only as a starting point for different discussions. At the same time, evolving international legal norms have come to engage with the duty to consult in new ways that may have further impact in the future. Between all of these developments, there are strong reasons for a revised edition in this tenth anniversary year of the *Haida Nation* decision.

As in the first edition, this book is in the first instance an attempt to clarify the duty to consult as a constitutional duty,[11] to offer some ap-

---

SCC 69, [2005] 3 S.C.R. 388.

7   *Rio Tinto Alcan* v. *Carrier Sekani Tribal Council*, 2010 SCC 43, [2010] 2 S.C.R. 650.

8   *Beckman* v. *Little Salmon/Carmacks First Nation*, 2010 SCC 53, [2010] 3 S.C.R. 103.

9 · *Quebec (Attorney General)* v. *Moses*, 2010 SCC 17, [2010] 1 S.C.R. 557.

10   *Behn* v. *Moulton Contracting Ltd.*, 2013 SCC 26.

11   In some cases, the duty to consult may be determined by the terms of particular agreements. The *Nisga'a Final Agreement* (27 Apr. 1999), for example, establishes consultation requirements on federal and provincial regulations or policies affecting wildlife and bird management in the Nass Valley (9:50, 9:53, 9:95, and 9:96), and on provincial decisions on traplines and guiding (9:76, 9:82, and 9:85): www.ainc-inac.gc.ca/pr/agr/nsga/nisdex_e.html. The *Tlicho Agreement* (25 Aug. 2003) also contains numerous provisions on consultation (see especially 7.5.5, 7.13.5, 10.7.1, 12.5.1, 12.5.11, 12.12.1, 13.2.1, 14.3.2, 14.5.1, 15.1.5, 16.6.1, 17.2.7(b), 17.5.5, 21.4.2, 22.2.13, 23.2, 23.3, 23.6, 25.2, and 26.3): www.ainc-inac.gc.ca/pr/agr/nwts/tliagr2_e.pdf. The Yukon Court of Appeal suggested in its Aug. 2008 decision in *Little Salmon/Carmacks First Nation* v. *Yukon (Minister of Energy, Mines, and Resources)* that "a duty to consult and accommodate applies in the interpretation of treaties and exists

proaches to understanding the developing case law at a deeper and more principled level, and to say something about possible future directions for the duty to consult in Canadian Aboriginal law. I hope this discussion remains of interest to those who want a better understanding of the duty to consult, and the opportunity to reflect on relevant developments in relation to it. The duty to consult has a fundamental importance for Aboriginal communities and organizations, for governments, industry stakeholders — indeed, all Canadians. Yet, even today, there has been less written on the duty to consult than its significance warrants.[12] Misunderstandings of the doctrine remain widespread.

At the same time, the duty to consult now arguably engages a more complex context than it originally did. The development of policy documents and other practices by various governments that take the duty to consult in new directions, by Aboriginal communities who seek to make the form of the duty more responsive to their community needs, and by industry stakeholders who seek to find ways to work practically within the law have all reshaped the actual effects of the doctrine in fascinating ways. In addition, ongoing developments within international law on Indigenous rights

---

independent of treaties." In that Court of Appeal decision, Kirkpatrick J.A., considering a government argument that the "certainty clause" in the *Little Salmon/Carmacks Final Agreement*, suggested that the agreement was intended to specify duties of consultation and thus precluded constitutional duties to consult on matters covered within the agreement; the constitutional duty to consult applies independently of the terms of a negotiated agreement. The subsequent Supreme Court of Canada decision in the case adopted a highly nuanced view in which treaty-based consultation provisions coexist with an always-present background constitutional duty.

12 The first edition was the first book-length treatment of the doctrine. Another is now Kirk N. Lambrecht, *Aboriginal Consultation, Environmental Assessment, and Regulatory Review in Canada* (Regina: Canadian Plains Research Centre, 2013), though it focuses more on the general context than on the detailed development of the doctrine. Every major Aboriginal law text of course now has significant discussion of the duty to consult. One of the best is Thomas Isaac, *Aboriginal Law: Commentary and Analysis* (Saskatoon: Purich Publishing, 2012). The duty to consult also enters into other kinds of discussions, such as in my recent broader book with some short perspectives on the duty to consult: Dwight Newman, *Natural Resource Jurisdiction in Canada* (Toronto: LexisNexis, 2013). And there are an increasing number of journal articles that discuss the duty to consult, something that was a genuinely limited literature at the time of the first edition.

have arguably changed the possible directions in which the duty is going or may go in future.

Individual readers may find different paths through this book; I welcome that, although I would suggest that there is an overall narrative flow and I would urge readers to consider that as well. The book begins from the fact that the *Haida Nation* trilogy and subsequent cases depart from earlier case law in elaborating the existence of a duty to consult Aboriginal communities potentially affected by government decision-making prior to final proof of an Aboriginal rights or Aboriginal title claim.[13] Although this duty had begun to be recognized in some lower courts before the Supreme Court of Canada recognized it,[14] the bulk of discussion around any consultation duties prior to this trilogy was in the much more limited context of the rules on infringement of established s. 35 rights.[15] The initial trilogy transformed the discourse of the duty to consult and fundamentally altered the steps that government agencies must take prior to making various decisions. In these cases, the Court also decided that the duty to consult is one owed specifically by governments,[16] not by third party corporate stakeholders, as some prior case law had suggested.[17] This decision shapes the duty in particular ways, although it does not diminish the impact of the duty on corporate stakeholders, particularly in the context of resource developments in traditional Aboriginal territories.[18] These cases, subsequent lower court decisions, and various groups' policy making have shaped the duty to consult.

The complex frameworks in which the duty to consult is under discussion have suggested a particular format for this book. In Chapter 1, I will turn to a fuller discussion of the duty to consult trilogy and the key holdings from those three cases — thus offering an introduction to the fundamental doctrinal content of the duty to consult — before turning

---

13 *Haida Nation, supra* note 4 at paras. 34–38.

14 See especially *Halfway River First Nation* v. *British Columbia (Minister of Forests)* (1999), 64 B.C.L.R. (3d) 206 (B.C.C.A.).

15 *Sparrow, supra* note 3 at para. 67.

16 *Haida Nation, supra* note 4 at para. 53.

17 *Ibid.* at paras. 53-56; *Haida Nation* v. *British Columbia (Minister of Forests)*, 2002 BCCA 462, 216 D.L.R. (4th) 1 at para. 73.

18 *Haida Nation, supra* note 4 at para. 53; *Taku River Tlingit, supra* note 5 at paras. 18, 46.

to key later developments and then, finally, to several possible theoretical approaches to understanding the duty to consult that integrate the main doctrinal features from the first sketch.

Chapters 2 and 3 examine the judicial doctrine of the duty to consult as developed in subsequent case law, addressing various more detailed features of or applications of the duty to consult. Chapter 4 explores the development of duty to consult policies by governments, industry stakeholders, and Aboriginal communities, arguing that their policies and practices further flesh out the law and also establish much of its practical significance. Chapter 5 examines some of the key developments in international law related to the duty, partly considering the comparative approaches of other states, and seeks to integrate this analysis with the theoretical approaches from the introductory chapter to offer some possibilities concerning future development of the duty to consult. The book thus seeks to further understanding of the doctrine on both a principled level and in terms of a more detailed examination of its development over the past ten years. I will argue that the detailed examination of doctrine, policy, and practice is essential for coming to terms with any theoretically oriented understandings of the duty to consult.

The duty to consult is of national importance for Canada in terms of the future directions of Aboriginal law and Aboriginal/non-Aboriginal relations. It is also of international importance as part of the ongoing development of systems to better protect the rights of Indigenous peoples. This book, then, is an act of scholarship relevant to those national and international contexts, but at the same time it is a work deeply rooted in place. Although the book discusses case law from across Canada, it would be confusing to write as if the duty to consult affected all parts of the country in the same way. The demographics of Canada and the location of our larger resource industries make this book particularly rooted in and relevant to a Western Canadian demographic and developmental context. This should not make the book any less relevant to those who live elsewhere, but make it richer for all.

The book has benefited from discussions over time with many different people and hopefully is responsive to different perspectives from that wide variety of contexts—whether legal theory discussion groups at universities, community members in duty to consult workshops with First Nations, Aboriginal leadership at resource development workshops, legal practitioners at various Canadian Bar Association events, judges from across the country at the National Judicial Institute, government officials at presentations to Crown corporations, industry stakeholders at international mining and energy conferences. I am grateful for all who have spoken with me about the duty to consult. Though this book treats the legal doctrine, it is more informed on its broader contexts due to these discussions. I hope that this book may foster and nurture further discussions of this important legal doctrine.

1

Introduction: Doctrine and Theory

1.1 Origins of the Duty to Consult

The duty to consult Aboriginal communities concerning potential impacts on their rights from government decisions is a proactive duty applying prior to a government taking action that may have those impacts. In that sense, it is a special protection for Aboriginal and treaty rights. Indeed, there would appear to be no such duty in the context of other rights, such as *Charter* rights.[1] The introduction of a duty to consult Aboriginal communities arguably reflects a particular response to historical imbalances of power and to the danger of severe impacts on Aboriginal communities from governments that often operate in very different cultural contexts, and with a limited sense of the implications of their actions on Aboriginal interests.

Those concerns are not unique to the Canadian context. Indeed, duties of consultation are not unique to Canada. Later parts of this book will engage with deeper complexities on the point, but duties of consultation comparable to those in Canada are increasingly present in the domestic law of other countries as well, and they are also present in developing international law norms on the rights of Indigenous peoples. Although there are more complex things to be said about its status in international law,

---

1   The idea has been argued in a major labour rights case that primarily concerns whether the *Charter of Rights* protects the right to strike, *Saskatchewan Federation of Labour* v. *Saskatchewan*, 2012 SKQB 62, revised on that issue in *R.* v. *Saskatchewan Federation of Labour*, 2013 SKCA 43, but the idea of a duty to consult prior to breaching any *Charter* rights was rejected at trial and at the Court of Appeal, though it could yet resurface at the Supreme Court of Canada.

the *Declaration on the Rights of Indigenous Peoples* (DRIP),[2] adopted by the United Nations General Assembly in 2007, crystallizes many principles on Indigenous rights in international law. Among its provisions are a number of Articles referring to obligations of consultation arising prior to impacts on Indigenous communities, to be considered at further length in Chapter 5 of this book. For now, the point is that the duty to consult does not exist in isolation in Canada, but stems from a broader international approach to improved interactions between states and Indigenous peoples.

In the Canadian context specifically, the duty to consult is associated with more localized concepts. The case law connects it with a concept known as the honour of the Crown as well as with the underlying objective of s. 35 of the *Constitution Act, 1982*, which the Supreme Court of Canada has interpreted purposively as aimed at promoting reconciliation. At the same time, the duty to consult inevitably carries out significant economic regulation in the context of natural resource developments. It is a multi-faceted concept.

Canadian references to the duty to consult in Aboriginal law contexts originate in some of the early post-1982 case law on s. 35 Aboriginal rights. Consultation was, though, even part of the fiduciary duty of the Crown in particular circumstances in the *Guerin* case in 1984, which was a common law case whose facts pre-dated the constitutional Aboriginal rights era.[3] It played an even larger role within the test developed in the *Sparrow* case, for when limits on s. 35 Aboriginal rights could be justified.[4] The idea of consultation was mentioned again in *Delgamuukw*.[5] Thus, the courts always recognized the possible protective potential of consultation. But its proactive dimension as a generalized requirement had not yet been established.

1.2 The 2004–2005 Supreme Court Trilogy

Whatever may be said about deeper historical origins to the modern duty to consult doctrine, any extended discussion of the duty to consult in Canadian law must ultimately start with the trilogy of cases that have trans-

---

2   *Declaration on the Rights of Indigenous Peoples*, G.A. Res. 61/295, U.N. Doc. A/RES/47/1 (2007).

3   *Guerin* v. *The Queen*, [1984] 2 S.C.R. 335.

4   *R.* v. *Sparrow*, [1990] 1 S.C.R. 1075.

5   *Delgamuukw* v. *British Columbia*, [1997] 3 S.C.R. 1010.

formed the field of discourse, particularly the *Haida Nation* decision, in which Chief Justice McLachlin set out the fundamental terms of the modern doctrine.[6] The issue was the government's replacement and transfer of a tree farm license to Weyerhaeuser, a large forestry corporation. The court held that the government ought to have consulted the Haida Nation prior to these actions, as the Crown is bound to act honourably in its relations with Aboriginal peoples.

According to the Supreme Court, this duty to consult arose even prior to a final proof of a claim in the courts or final resolution of the claim through a negotiated settlement.[7] It was precisely because the final shape of Aboriginal rights and title had not yet been established that it was important for governments to consult with the Aboriginal community so as not to affect their interests detrimentally during the process of proving and resolving a claim. The modern duty to consult doctrine thus creates a proactive duty on governments in the face of uncertainty. Doing so offers some core protection to Aboriginal rights, even where they have not yet been definitively established. Somewhat ironically, although the duty to consult ultimately depends upon underlying rights, the procedural protection that it affords may actually be more of a protection than any attempt at litigation over the rights themselves.

A legal duty to consult, wrote McLachlin, "arises when the Crown has knowledge, real or constructive, of the potential existence of the Aboriginal right or title and contemplates conduct that might adversely affect it."[8] The content was to be defined based on a spectrum that takes into account the strength of the claim and the seriousness of the potential adverse impact on the right or title claimed.[9] Contrary to the conclusion of the Court of Appeal in the case, the Supreme Court of Canada held that the duty is one owed by the Crown only, due to its duties of honour, and not by third parties such as the forestry company.[10]

In *Haida Nation*, the impact of forestry on the Haida was serious, and the government had not consulted the community beforehand. The Su-

---

6   *Haida Nation* v. *British Columbia (Minister of Forests)*, 2004 SCC 73, [2004] 3 S.C.R. 511.

7   *Ibid.* at paras. 31, 32, 76.

8   *Ibid.* at para. 35.

9   *Ibid.* at paras. 43-45.

10 *Ibid.* at para. 53.

preme Court concluded that it had breached its duties and needed to consider significant accommodation.[11] In the companion case, *Taku River Tlingit First Nation*,[12] the Supreme Court ultimately concluded that the government had met the consultation requirements through an environmental assessment.[13] The case arose from a mining company's application to reopen an old mine in northwestern British Columbia; the company hoped to build a 160-km road to the mine through traditional Taku River Tlingit territory. The Tlingit raised concerns about the possible impacts on wildlife and other traditional uses, as well as their title claim. Although the potentially serious impacts implied some depth to the consultation,[14] there was a significant consideration of Aboriginal claims, including strategies on wildlife migration and the management and closure of the road. The court concluded that the government had met its duty.[15]

The *Mikisew Cree* case[16] extended this doctrine to treaty rights, subject to appropriate modifications.[17] The case arose following protests by the Mikisew Cree against the location of a winter road near their reserve on Treaty 8 lands in northern Alberta. The Cree argued that this road would affect their traditional lifestyle because it crossed a number of trap lines and hunting grounds. Where the Minister planned to "take up" lands under the treaty for the purpose of this road, the Supreme Court of Canada held that there was an obligation to consult in order to ensure that there was an honourable process in the "taking up" of these lands.[18] In this case, there had not been adequate consultation, and Justice Binnie's judgement sent the Crown back to deal with the project in light of the reasons elaborated in the judgement.[19] The duty to consult thus arises in relation to government

---

11   *Ibid.* at paras. 76, 79.

12   *Taku River Tlingit First Nation* v. *British Columbia (Project Assessment Director)*, 2003 SCC 74, [2004] 3 S.C.R. 550.

13   *Ibid.* at paras. 22, 47.

14   *Ibid.* at para. 32.

15   *Ibid.* at para. 41.

16   *Mikisew Cree First Nation* v. *Canada (Minister of Canadian Heritage)*, 2005 SCC 69, [2005] 3 S.C.R.388.

17   *Ibid.* at paras. 63, 32-34, 51-56.

18   *Ibid.* at para. 59.

19   *Ibid.* at para. 69.

actions that have potential impacts on treaty rights.[20] Obviously, what is known to the government in terms of the content of the right involved is more substantial in the context of treaty rights, thus rendering parts of the basic test less relevant.[21] Subject to the resulting modification, however, the duty to consult arises in the context of treaty rights on an approach parallel to that in the Aboriginal rights or title context.[22]

In these cases, the Supreme Court established a new legal doctrine — indeed, a new realm of Aboriginal law. What began with a simple tree farm license led to the need to understand a new legal framework in relation to Aboriginal rights, title, and treaty rights. This book seeks to offer readers an understanding of this area by going beyond the basics of the Supreme Court of Canada's three initial cases.

1.3 Recent Supreme Court Cases and Emerging Issues

After these three initial cases, the Supreme Court did not revisit the duty to consult for some time. Although there were attempts to get cases there on appeal, the Supreme Court chose to grant leave on an appeal and weigh in once again on the duty to consult only in 2010. By then, certain issues had emerged as needing resolution from the highest court. These included issues related to the role of various administrative bodies in implementing the duty to consult, issues related to how the duty to consult interacted with historic breaches, and issues related to the duty to consult in the context of modern treaties.

The *Rio Tinto* case in 2010 was the Court's opportunity to speak to the first two of these issues.[23] The case concerned applications for renewals of energy production deals at hydroelectric facilities powered by dams that had been built decades prior, without consultation and with obvious impacts on Aboriginal communities in the area. Issues were raised concerning what role a utilities commission should play in relation to the duty to consult, as well as whether any consultation obligation could arise in the context of the renewal.

---

20   *Ibid.* at para. 67.

21   *Ibid.* at para. 34.

22   *Ibid.* at paras. 33, 44.

23   *Rio Tinto Alcan* v. *Carrier Sekani Tribal Council*, 2010 SCC 43, [2010] 2 S.C.R. 650.

The role of a utilities commission vis-à-vis the duty to consult may seem like it was one context-specific question. But it represented a broader set of questions about what role administrative boards and tribunals have in seeing that the duty to consult is fulfilled, or assessing whether it has been. A modern democratic government involves many different administrative authorities. Justice LeBel of the Supreme Court once colourfully described this variety:

> At first glance, labour boards, police commissions, and milk control boards may seem to have about as much in common as assembly lines, cops, and cows! Administrative bodies do, of course, have some common features, but the diversity of their powers, mandate and structure is such that to apply particular standards from one context to another might well be entirely inappropriate.[24]

But all the administrative decisions that these different entities make can potentially raise duty to consult issues. The question was what role the board or tribunal itself played in addressing those.

The Court responded in *Rio Tinto* essentially by referencing the variety of mandates placed upon different governmental administrative bodies. It states quite simply that "[t]he duty on a tribunal to consider consultation and the scope of that inquiry depends on the mandate conferred by the legislation that creates the tribunal."[25] Some tribunals can actually be set up to be responsible to carry out consultation. Some can be set up to assess consultation carried out by others. And some have no role in consultation. In the last case, the duty to consult does not disappear. The government is always obligated to organize itself so that the legally required consultation occurs somehow. The courts simply will not dictate that form of organization, and the government's statutory mandates for each administrative board or tribunal determine what that particular part of government does.

The Court also expressed limits on the role of the duty to consult in its *Rio Tinto* decision,[26] resolving another issue that had been lingering. According to the Court in the decision, the duty to consult is not meant to ad-

---

24   *Blencoe* v. *British Columbia (Human Rights Commission)*, 2000 SCC 44, [2000] 2 S.C.R. 307, at para. 158.

25   *Rio Tinto, supra* note 23 at para. 55.

26   *Rio Tinto, supra* note 23.

dress historic issues but is a forward-looking duty that attaches to potential future impacts of decisions being made today. If there is a failure to consult, there can be a challenge to that failure which seeks consultation during an interim period after the failure of consultation. But, if consultation is not pursued, then any breach of rights ultimately transforms into a past breach that is subject to challenge based on the underlying substantive doctrine of Aboriginal and treaty rights rather than based on a procedural mechanism that has forward-looking purposes. The duty to consult achieves many things, but it is not intended to replace all Aboriginal and treaty rights jurisprudence.

Also in 2010, the Supreme Court addressed certain specific questions regarding to what extent the duty to consult continues to coexist with more specifically articulated consultation obligations in modern treaties that some then thought were meant to replace the general duty to consult doctrine. In the *Moses* case,[27] a much more specific case about the *James Bay Agreement*, and the more generalizable *Little Salmon* case,[28] the Supreme Court struck a sort of middle path on this issue. Although the consultation requirements in carefully negotiated, highly detailed modern treaties will largely define consultation in relation to those treaties, the background duty to consult does not entirely disappear. It is always a background constitutional consideration that serves an ultimate protective function.

Most recently, in 2013, the Supreme Court was confronted with arguments that there might be a duty to consult with Aboriginal individuals who hold rights, rather than simply with rights-bearing communities. The duty to consult had always previously been thought to be owed only to communities. The possibility of a duty owed in some circumstances to individuals arose in *Behn* v. *Moulton Contracting.*[29] This case concerned a situation where some community members differed from the community's position and took it upon themselves to launch a roadblock, defending their actions on the basis that they had not been individually consulted. These facts, of course, were not especially sympathetic, as the courts do not wish to be seen to be authorizing individual self-help actions. But some arguing in the case, including particularly the Grand Council of the Crees,

---

27 *Quebec (Attorney General)* v. *Moses*, 2010 SCC 17, [2010] 1 S.C.R. 557.

28 *Beckman* v. *Little Salmon/Carmacks First Nation*, 2010 SCC 53, [2010] 3 S.C.R. 103.

29 *Behn* v. *Moulton Contracting Ltd.*, 2013 SCC 26.

took it as a case to raise the possibility of individually held Aboriginal rights distinct from the rights typically considered to be held communally.[30] The Court did not reject this argument, but it did not accept it, either. It remains something to be considered in future, and it raises many complex considerations.

The case law of recent years has left several other big questions open. First, a further dimension of the *Rio Tinto* case[31] was that it affirmed a principle from previous lower court case law that the duty to consult can be engaged at an early, strategic stage of decision-making.[32] The requirement to consult on strategic, high-level decisions flows logically from the idea that the duty to consult is engaged when a decision is made that has the potential to affect Aboriginal or treaty rights adversely. If the strategic decision effectively determines later decisions, then it may be important that there be consultation on it if consultation is to be meaningful. However, just what this means raises many complexities, and there is ongoing lower court case law that is grappling with it; this will be the subject of discussion later in the book.

While the Court in *Rio Tinto* was ready to specifically state that strategic decisions can engage the duty to consult, it went out of its way to raise and then leave for a future day the question of whether legislative action can engage the duty to consult.[33] The question of whether the duty to consult applies to legislative action is a major question, with significant implications, to which this book will return. If international law developments on the duty to consult filter through, Article 19 of the DRIP does refer to a duty to consult on legislative action[34] — but the legal status of such

---

30   *Ibid.* at paras. 34-35.

31   *Rio Tinto, supra* note 23.

32   *Ibid.* at para. 44. The Court writes here that "the duty to consult extends to 'strategic, higher level decisions' that may have an impact on Aboriginal claims and rights."

33   *Ibid.* The Court ends the paragraph with the unnecessary statement that "[w]e leave for another day the question of whether government conduct includes legislative action": see *R. v. Lefthand*, 2007 ABCA 206, 77 Alta. L.R. (4th) 203, at paras. 37-40.

34   *Declaration on the Rights of Indigenous Peoples, supra* note 2, art. 19 states as follows: "States shall consult and cooperate in good faith with the indigenous peoples concerned through their own representative institutions in order to obtain their free, prior and informed consent before adopting and imple-

provisions requires more discussion. For now, the issue is worth flagging simply as a major unresolved question — one that the Supreme Court has deliberately left as such.

A recent decision of the Supreme Court to deny leave to appeal in the *Ross River Dena Council* case[35] bears to some extent on this question, and, more generally, opens possible new facets of the duty to consult. In the case, an Aboriginal community that claimed to be affected by preliminary exploration activity challenged Yukon's long-standing free entry mining regime. Under that regime, someone could stake a claim and then had a right under statute to have that claim automatically registered, which permitted some limited activities. The Yukon Court of Appeal held that the government had to redesign the system so as to create a role for consultation at an earlier stage than the legislation effectively established. In other words, it said that the existence of the duty to consult did not just apply to an administrative decision under an existing statute, but mandated a significant change to the statute itself. This decision changes the scope of the duty to consult. That the Supreme Court denied an opportunity to appeal the decision may say only that it does not yet wish to consider the issue. But it left in place a decision that is a tremendously interesting precedent that could change the very scope of the duty to consult.

1.4 Theoretical Approaches to the Duty to Consult

The rights recognized and affirmed by s. 35 of the *Constitution Act, 1982* — which now includes the duty to consult — are not specified by the written text of the Constitution. In some senses, then, the definition of s. 35 rights has been left to negotiations and to the courts. This is not owing to a lack of content to s. 35. Indeed, s. 35 merely "recognized and affirmed" rights that existed prior to European settlement and had, in many respects, ongoing status in the common law, even if not always effectively recognized.[36] How-

---

menting legislative or administrative measures that may affect them."

35   *Ross River Dena Council* v. *Government of Yukon*, 2012 YKCA 13, leave to appeal to Supreme Court of Canada denied 19 September 2013.

36   See Kent McNeil, *Common Law Aboriginal Title* (Oxford: Clarendon, 1989); and Brian Slattery, "Understanding Aboriginal Rights" (1987) 66 Can. Bar Rev. 727. Slattery offers a powerful conception of the nature of Aboriginal rights as arising intersocietally from the onset of encounter among different communities.

ever, uncertainties around the form and scope of these pre-existing rights, combined with the complex cross-cultural interaction of concepts,[37] have given rise to ongoing instability in Canada's constitutional law regarding Aboriginal rights, with concepts sometimes shifting rapidly in the space of a few years.[38]

This lack of stability is not surprising in constitutional law. In determining what a limited set of cases mean in the context of a case before the court, judges will consider the underlying meaning of the constitutional norms at issue, often in terms of the underlying theoretical scope of the concepts and a normative conception of the rights. So, for instance, a judge confronting an innovative factual case concerned with freedom of expression will consider not only the direct application of prior case law but also the underlying normative conceptualization of freedom of expression that this case law embodies. This is not to say that the judge has any duty other than to apply the law; it is to say, rather, that the content of the law is rich with meaning and a judge must work with this. There is, of course, a much longer-standing and larger body of normative analysis on the meaning of concepts such as freedom of expression than on the complex intersocietal concepts arising in the s. 35 context, which gives rise to ongoing challenges in applying the section in a consistent and principled manner.

Judges are developing the body of thought in this area in the complex context of cross-cultural legal, normative, and political encounters. An important question is, on what normative conceptualizations of the duty to consult judges or others needing to interpret the law are to draw when faced with a novel legal question in a factual context unlike those that have come before. In such cases, judges must consider not just the determinate rules from prior cases but also the broader principles that these rules embody and instantiate.[39] Only by developing, with appropriate prudence

---

37   See Dwight G. Newman, "You Still Know Nothin' 'Bout Me: Toward Cross-Cultural Theorizing of Aboriginal Rights" (2007) 52 McGill L.J. 725.

38   For an interesting discussion of the shifts in Aboriginal title jurisprudence, see Kent McNeil, "Aboriginal Title and the Supreme Court: What's Happening?" (2006) 69 Sask. L. Rev. 281; see also Dwight G. Newman, "Prior Occupation and Schismatic Principles: Toward a Normative Theorization of Aboriginal Title" (2007) 44 Alta. L.Rev. 779.

39   This description of the content of the law is coherent with Ronald Dworkin's *Taking Rights Seriously* (London: Duckworth, 1978). Dworkin has in more recent works offered a more extended account, suggesting that decision-making

and modesty, a broader theory of the law is it possible to address previously unanswered questions within the law.

One might suggest that the judges, in the duty to consult context, simply draw on a longstanding concept of the "honour of the Crown,"[40] but this does not displace the need to develop a broader theoretical account of the duty to consult in order to understand it. The early doctrinal foundations of the "honour of the Crown" consist of a concept that gave rise to a principle of interpretation that Crown grants should be interpreted in a manner such that they were not void.[41] Without further development of the concept, this doctrine has no immediate application in the context of the duty to consult. To understand the duty to consult, it is necessary to probe potentially deeper theoretical accounts. It would be imprudent to characterize the duty to consult before a careful analysis of the existing jurisprudence, but it is also important to set out some possibilities in order to consider them carefully while proceeding through the more doctrinal discussion.

To understand the duty to consult doctrine in a deeper sense, then, it is valuable to go behind the judgements to the more fundamental principles the duty to consult furthers. Doing so provides a set of possible lenses for looking at the case law and evaluating each case as to how successfully it advances the doctrine's underlying purposes. It also enables an estimation of likely future directions of the duty. Particularly in the case of areas of law that are not fully defined by existing determinations of legal doctrine — such as in the context of Aboriginal rights protected by s. 35 of the Constitution — there is both a need to refer to existing doctrine and a need to go to the theoretical foundations of these areas to understand the law and its future development.

In terms of the basic doctrine from the Supreme Court of Canada's initial trilogy, to begin to distinguish among the fit of different theories of the

---

in each particular case must consider the two elements of a decision's fit with existing jurisprudence and its moral soundness, thus bridging positivism's close definition of legal content and natural law's emphasis on the justness of law. See Dworkin's *Law's Empire* (Cambridge: Belknap, 1986) and *Justice in Robes* (Cambridge: Harvard University Press, 2006).

40   See, for example, *Haida Nation*, *supra* note 6 at para. 16.

41   Roger Earl of Rutland's Case (1608), 8 Co. Rep. 55a at 56a-b, 77 E.R. 555 at 557; the Case of the Churchwardens of St. Saviour in Southwark (1613), 10 Co. Rep. 66b a 67b, 77 E.R. 1025 at 1027.

doctrine, it is worth noting five fundamental components of the duty to consult as developed in those cases:

1. the duty to consult arises prior to proof of an Aboriginal rights or title claim or in the context of uncertain effects on a treaty right;[42]

2. the duty to consult is triggered relatively easily, based on an insufficient level of knowledge on the part of the Crown relative to a possible claim with which government action potentially interferes;[43]

3. the strength or scope of the duty to consult in particular circumstances lies along a spectrum of possibilities, with a richer consultation requirement arising from a stronger *prima facie* Aboriginal claim and/or a more serious impact on the underlying Aboriginal right or treaty right;[44]

4. within this spectrum, the duty ranges from a minimal notice requirement to a duty to carry out some degree of accommodation of the Aboriginal interests, but it does not include an Aboriginal power of veto over any particular decision;[45] and

5. failure to meet a duty to consult can lead to a range of remedies, from an injunction against a particular government action altogether (or, in some instance, damages) but, more commonly, an order to carry out the consultation prior to proceeding.[46]

The most commonly advanced theoretical foundation for the duty to consult doctrine is that provided by the Court itself as an explanation of the grounding of the doctrine, with McLachlin C.J.C. explaining in *Haida Nation* that the "government's duty to consult with Aboriginal peoples and accommodate their interests is grounded in the honour of the Crown."[47] Her discussion of the honour of the Crown encompasses, in adjacent text,

---

42   *Haida Nation, supra* note 6 at paras. 35-36; *Mikisew Cree First Nation, supra* note 16 at paras. 33-34.

43   *Haida Nation, ibid.* at para. 35.

44   *Ibid.* at paras. 43-45; *Taku River Tlingit First Nation, supra* note 12 at para. 32.

45   *Haida Nation, supra* note 6 at para. 48.

46   *Ibid.* at paras. 13-14

47   *Ibid.* at para. 16.

a discussion of the idea that the honour of the Crown also embodies such related principles as that the Crown should not engage in "sharp dealing" in making or interpreting treaties,[48] potentially suggesting a somewhat attenuated version of the content of the honour at stake.

Nonetheless, there is a legal obligation on governments arising from the principle that the Crown must act in accordance with a particular virtue — namely, honour. The concept of the Crown, of course, is symbolic, with the underlying foundation amounting to a claim that a settler people in ongoing encounter with Indigenous peoples must deal honourably with them and, more generally, act in accordance with the virtue of honour.

The idea that the honour of the Crown fundamentally characterizes Crown obligations to Aboriginal peoples is important to understand. The Supreme Court has actually in recent years signalled that the honour of the Crown concept is going to be the main concept that defines Crown obligations. In some early cases, it had seemed like the courts were going to make extensive use of the idea of fiduciary duties to Aboriginal communities. But the recent case law definitively rejects any wide use of that concept and restricts it to a narrow area, something made extraordinarily clear in the recent *Manitoba Métis Federation* decision.[49] Some writing has not yet drawn a clear distinction between the concepts or made fully clear the shift from fiduciary duty to honour of the Crown.[50] A recent LL.M. thesis from the University of Saskatchewan College of Law written by Jamie Dickson examines very thoroughly the whole history of this shift and why the courts have made this shift, and it is to be hoped that he publishes it so that its discussion is more widely available.[51]

The idea of honour of the Crown has not necessarily become more clearly defined, even though it is the doctrinal — and perhaps the theor-

---

48   *Ibid.* at paras. 19-20.

49   *Manitoba Métis Federation Inc.* v. *Canada (Attorney General)*, 2013 SCC 14, [2013] 1 S.C.R. 623.

50   This is true of much Aboriginal law writing, including even to some extent of works that appeared to be trying to decipher them but still saw fiduciary duties as a larger concept than they now appear to be. See e.g. Timothy Mc-Cabe, *The Honour of the Crown and its Fiduciary Duties to Aboriginal Peoples* (Toronto: LexisNexis Canada, 2008).

51   Jamie Dickson, "The Honour of the Crown: Making Sense of Crown Liability Doctrine in Crown/Aboriginal Law in Canada" (LL.M. thesis, University of Saskatchewan College of Law, 2013).

etical — source of not only the duty to consult but also other Crown duties such as are discussed in *Manitoba Métis Federation*.[52] When the *Haida Nation* court picked up the concept, it wittingly or unwittingly drew on a concept that has deep roots in Aboriginal cultural contexts as well. Many Aboriginal communities have deep concepts of honour, but they may read the term in different ways than the Canadian courts do. The concept is certainly now richer than in the ancient English case law. But some writers have tried to read forward old English case law on the concept more substantially — for example, during his time as Treaty Commissioner, David Arnot wrote a major piece that attempted to do so and he continues those efforts in further writing.[53] The honour of the Crown concept is going to be subject to further clarification and elaboration over time. But, in the meantime, it is now clearly a leading concept in Aboriginal law even without that full elaboration as yet.

Treating the honour of the Crown as a possible theoretical approach underlying the duty to consult, this approach can fit readily into some of the features of the duty to consult doctrine. It fits easily enough with the claim that governments must consult with Aboriginal peoples about unproven claims, for the undermining of an Aboriginal right while it is stalled in litigation or negotiation would be dishonourable. Similarly, the easy triggering of the duty to consult fits with a plausible conception of honour. Our conception of honour needs to be reasonably fulsome, for if we acknowledge that one of its central characteristics is a prohibition against sharp dealing, sharp dealing on the application of the concept itself cannot be permitted. On this component, though, the spectrum of duties potentially embraced by the duty to consult in particular circumstances becomes more difficult to justify. To suppose that it is stronger in some circumstances and weaker in others does not sit easily with an effort to ensure that (honourable) dealing is above reproach. Indeed, it arguably appears to contain more of a weighing of costs and benefits than any conceptions of honour will contain.

This realization leads us directly to a second possible theoretical ap-

---

52   *Manitoba Métis Federation, supra* note 49.

53   David M. Arnot, "The Honour of the Crown" (1996) 60 Sask. L. Rev. 339; David Arnot, "The Honour of First Nations — The Honour of the Crown: The Unique Relationship of First Nations with the Crown," in Jennifer Smith & D. Michael Jackson (Eds.), *The Evolving Canadian Crown* (Kingston: McGill-Queen's University Press, 2012).

proach to the duty to consult, one to which the Court adverts in *Haida Nation*, although less explicitly. Prior to discussing the duty to consult in *Haida Nation*, the Court considered first whether to grant an interlocutory injunction until there was a resolution of the Aboriginal rights case. Chief Justice McLachlin dismissed the possibility:

> An interlocutory injunction over such a long period of time might work unnecessary prejudice and may diminish incentives on the part of the successful party to compromise. While Aboriginal claims can be and are pursued through litigation, negotiation is a preferable way of reconciling state and Aboriginal interests. For all these reasons, interlocutory injunctions may fail to adequately take account of Aboriginal interests prior to their final determination.[54]

This dismissal is part of the grounding for the duty to consult doctrine that the Court elaborates later in the judgement, implicitly constituting part of the justification for this latter doctrine. This justification, then, is implicitly that the duty to consult doctrine — as compared to an approach founded on interlocutory injunctions during litigation or negotiation — fosters appropriate incentives for negotiation and is thus preferable on the grounds of what will promote the best negotiation processes among Aboriginal and non-Aboriginal communities, thus calling for attention to a certain kind of consequence of the doctrinal framework.

In one sense, this theoretical explanation of the doctrine would assert the responsibility of the courts to cast the "shadow of the law" — which is sometimes described as what shape it puts on negotiation contexts[55] — to facilitate something desirable within the negotiation process. This kind of explanation, of course, does not have to say that the proper analysis of the duty to consult in specific circumstances is that which facilitates the best negotiation process or outcome in those particular circumstances. The courts' rationale for promoting negotiation in the Aboriginal law context — a not infrequently expressed preference[56] — is, in part, that they lack sig-

---

54 *Haida Nation, supra* note 6 at para. 14.

55 The term originates with Robert H. Mnookin & Lewis Kornhauser, "Bargaining in the Shadow of the Law: The Case of Divorce" (1979) 88 Yale L.J. 950.

56 See Dwight G. Newman, "Negotiated Rights Enforcement" (2006) 69 Sask. L. Rev. 119.

nificant information that the parties can best bring to bear on a particular Aboriginal rights negotiation.[57]

Lacking full information about particular circumstances and promoting negotiation for precisely this reason, the courts might then easily promote negotiation through a structuring of such contexts through the creation of appropriate incentives for the parties themselves.

This theoretical approach to the duty to consult fits more readily with the notion of a spectrum. The structuring of negotiation will be dependent on the circumstances that give rise to claims for greater or lesser bargaining power by the different parties. It is appropriate that Aboriginal communities with relatively stronger *prima facie* claims, or whose claims are more seriously affected, have greater power in the relevant negotiation processes. This theoretical approach thus more readily explains the spectrum analysis within the duty to consult.

It can be argued, however, that it sits less easily with the notion of an easy triggering of the duty to consult. On this theoretical approach, the notion of the spectrum within the duty to consult is one advancing a structuring of negotiations in accordance with relevant moral considerations. An Aboriginal rights claim of little *prima facie* strength in the context of a near-trivial impact on the community would arguably not give rise to a moral reason to create any bargaining power at all for the Aboriginal community, yet the duty to consult doctrine would nonetheless create some rights, if only at a minimal level.[58]

Perhaps more significantly, a theoretical approach based on these kinds of result-oriented considerations would speak to an element that is not present in the duty to consult — namely, a limitation of the duty to consult in some circumstances where limitations would be justified on an appropriate cost-benefit analysis. (The argument for a less easy triggering of the duty is actually a special case of this broader point.) If there were specifiable circumstances in which the introduction of a duty to consult would skew negotiations in a manner that promoted inefficiency, a results-oriented account of the doctrine would lean toward taking account of these circumstances in the form of further limits on the doctrine. So, for example, circumstances in which governments wished to develop certain

---

57 *Ibid.*

58 Just to be clear at this juncture, I do speak of the doctrine only as enunciated in *Haida Nation.* Some lower courts have been more ready to apply internal limits to when the duty to consult is triggered.

lands for significant economic development purposes would, on this account, reasonably give rise to a more attenuated duty to consult in relation to proposed government activities on those lands.

A third theoretical approach to the duty to consult would see it as a doctrine promoting "reconciliation" — itself a complex and contested concept in Aboriginal law, as I have discussed elsewhere,[59] but one not easily described as a result because it is often seen more in terms of a process.

This theoretical approach would, like the others, find some basis in the text of the *Haida Nation* judgement:

> Honourable negotiation implies a duty to consult with Aboriginal claimants and conclude an honourable agreement reflecting the claimants' inherent rights. But proving rights may take time, sometimes a very long time. In the meantime, how are the interests under discussion to be treated? Underlying this question is the need to reconcile prior Aboriginal occupation of the land with the reality of Crown sovereignty. Is the Crown, under the aegis of its asserted sovereignty, entitled to use the resources at issue as it chooses, pending proof and resolution of the Aboriginal claim? Or must it adjust its conduct to reflect the as yet unresolved rights claimed by the Aboriginal claimants?[60]

Within this account, then, the duty to consult is posited as a doctrine encapsulating a just reconciliation between the Crown and Aboriginal peoples in the context of unproven claims.[61] The duty to consult is an adjustment of government conduct to reflect unresolved claims, as part of a reconciliation of prior Aboriginal occupation and current Crown sovereignty.

Specific formulations of this account might potentially collapse into one of the other accounts,[62] but this account could be described as related to

---

59   Dwight Newman, "Reconciliation: Legal Conception(s) and Faces of Justice," in John Whyte (Ed.), *Moving Toward Justice* (Saskatoon: Purich, 2008).

60   *Haida Nation, supra* note 6 at para. 26.

61   See also the statement of Phelan J. in *Dene Tha' First Nation* v. *Canada (Minister of Environment)*, 2006 aff'd, 2008 FCA 20, 378 N.R. 251 FC 1354, [2007] 1 C.N.L.R. 1 at para. 82: "The goal of consultation is not to be narrowly interpreted as the mitigation of adverse effects on Aboriginal rights and/or title" (going on to state that the underlying goal of the doctrine is reconciliation).

62   One could argue, for example, that honourable dealings will best promote

a more generalized account of just relations among communities in the context of unresolved claims among those communities, or as striking a sort of balance between rights claims in the context of uncertainties about those claims. It could conceivably be situated within broader accounts of just relations between communities or within broader accounts related to rights conflicts. There would, thus, clearly be more that one could develop within this account, for several possible versions are implicit within it. Indeed, without that further development, it faces a danger of being able to provide relatively limited guidance on implications for the doctrine. That said, something like this will obviously fit with some elements of the doctrine, with it following reasonably that an account of just relations between and among communities and/or rights conflicts between them will properly become involved in analysis based on a relatively low standard for the triggering of the duty to consult, and that the scope of the duty that mediates between the communities will then be adjusted to the circumstances of the relationship in the context of a particular rights conflict. To say this, however, is to submerge a larger set of questions concerning the details of this theoretical account that do not surface as easily from the text itself. For present purposes, however, I will leave it at that, and say that some such account could plausibly emerge in a more detailed form.

A fourth possible theoretical approach to the duty to consult, different again, would see the judicial development of a duty to consult as exemplifying and fostering what some would assert to be a broader normative commitment of Aboriginal law — namely, that it promote what Slattery terms a "generative constitutional order."[63] Such a theoretical approach would, as Slattery describes it, see "section 35 as serving a dynamic and not simply static function."[64] Parts of the *Haida Nation* judgement appear to situate the duty to consult within this kind of dynamic process:

---

reconciliation and thus arrive back at the first theory. That said, such moves might not seem the most plausible. There is a difference in orientation between asking the government to act in accord with a virtue of honour and asking the government to act in accord with a value of reconciliation.

63   Brian Slattery, "Aboriginal Rights and the Honour of the Crown" (2005) 29 S.C.L.R. (2d) 433, and "The Generative Structure of Aboriginal Rights" (2007) 38 S.C.L.R. (2d) 1.

64   Slattery, "Aboriginal Rights and the Honour of the Crown," *ibid.* at 440.

[T]he duty to consult and accommodate is part of a process of fair dealing and reconciliation that begins with the assertion of sovereignty and continues beyond formal claims resolution. Reconciliation is not a final legal remedy in the usual sense. Rather it is a process flowing from rights guaranteed by s. 35(1). . . . .[65]

This account of the duty to consult would see it as promoting an ongoing process of reconciliation. Concerned with an ethic of ongoing relationships, it would fit with some elements of the doctrine, notably the circumstances in which it arises and the preference for remedies for violations that promote ongoing negotiations. This account would also ground an unlimited doctrine, one not completed at any particular moment in the context of an ongoing relationship. However, the notion of the spectrum within the duty to consult doctrine is that a duty to consult can in some circumstances be successfully fulfilled without an ongoing course of consultations. So, again, there are ways in which this possible foundation of the duty to consult doctrine fits more and less well.

Each of these theories more readily fits some aspects of the doctrine than others. The obvious implication is that each, if adopted as a more definitive theoretical foundation, would push elements of the doctrine in different directions. To take one example in the elements already under discussion, an honour-oriented account would minimize the role of the spectrum analysis within the doctrine, whereas a results-oriented account would tend to expand it.

The different theoretical accounts will have different implications, as well, for questions not explicitly addressed thus far. Initial pronouncements on the modern duty to consult have tended to limit its application explicitly to Crown decisions and, implicitly, decisions concerning Crown lands.

Lower court case law has in some instances reawakened questions about the implications of the duty to consult for decisions related to privately owned lands, in light of suggestions in some of this lower court case law that there remains more to be said about the implications of Aboriginal title for privately owned lands.[66] The different theoretical approaches to the

---

65 *Haida Nation*, *supra* note 6 at para. 32, cited by Slattery, *ibid.*

66 Some of this suggestion was present in the trial court decision in *Tsilhqot'in Nation* v. *British Columbia*, 2007 BCSC 1700, [2008] 1 C.N.L.R. 112, 163 A.C.W.S. (3d) 873. For discussion, see Dwight Newman & Danielle Schweitzer, "Between Reconciliation and the Rule(s) of Law: *Tsilhqot'in Nation* v.

duty to consult potentially lead in significantly different directions on such questions. At the very least, they lead to entirely different analyses; given that, it might be surprising if they led to the same outcomes. An open-ended fostering of a generative constitutional order would presumably be favourable toward an expansion of the generative scope of the constitutional order. An approach concerned with reconciliation might look to the effects of opening such questions on prospects for reconciliation. A results-oriented account would look to the effects on negotiation contexts, likely having concerns with the uncertainties created for private landowners. An honour-oriented account would look to the overall honour of Canada's dealings with Aboriginal peoples, and would potentially be more sympathetic to the prospect of this development. These descriptions of likely attitudes are, of course, tentative, in that one could pursue significantly more work within each of these accounts to flesh out the account and its implications for this scenario. But they are sufficient to reinforce the likelihood that these different underlying accounts lead in different directions on controversial questions concerning the duty to consult.

The potential instability in the law relative to different theoretical underpinnings for it speaks to one reason we might have for seeking a more definitive theoretical account of the duty to consult doctrine. Although theoretical argument has been a major driver in Supreme Court of Canada case law on Aboriginal rights, particularly in the context of s. 35, in many different s. 35 contexts there are these remaining sorts of uncertainties in relation to theoretical underpinnings, and these uncertainties may be a possible explanation of some of the kinds of dramatic shifts we have seen in some areas of Aboriginal law through the post-1982 period. In some senses, then, the particular example of theorizing the duty to consult presents a subset of the challenges in theorizing Aboriginal law more generally.

It is important to recognize the presence in the duty to consult case law of several distinct theoretical foundations for the doctrine, some of

---

British Columbia" (2008) 42 U.B.C. L. Rev. 249. The *Tsilhqot'in Nation* trial judgement's uncertainties around private property issues have already influenced a later duty to consult decision in *Hupacasath First Nation v. British Columbia (Minister of Forests)*, 2008 BCSC 1505, [2009] 1 C.N.L.R. 30. What comes of some of this discussion may be significantly impacted by the Supreme Court of Canada ruling in the *Tsilhqot'in Nation* case heard in November 2013 and under reserve as of this writing.

the inconsistencies between them and their implications, and some of the interactions with the more general domain of theorizing Aboriginal law. Coming closer to answers on the theoretical foundation for the duty to consult will depend on further discussion of more detailed elements of the doctrine, more examples of its applications by lower courts that are actually putting it into practice, and the development of practices and policies by various stakeholders.

2

Legal Parameters of the Duty to Consult

2.1 Introduction

The Supreme Court of Canada's case law has specifically said that its consideration of the duty to consult has been partial and is to leave room for development of the doctrine by the lower courts. As Chief Justice McLachlin described it in *Haida Nation*,

> This case is the first of its kind to reach this Court. Our task is the modest one of establishing a general framework for the duty to consult and accommodate ... before Aboriginal title or rights have been decided. As this framework is applied, courts, in the age old tradition of the common law, will be called on to fill in the details of the duty to consult and accommodate.[1]

Justice Donald of the British Columbia Court of Appeal has recognized the lower courts' role in taking up this task, writing in a judgement of the case in question as "one of those cases foreseen by the Supreme Court of Canada ... where the broad general principles of the Crown's duty to consult and, if necessary, accommodate Aboriginal interests are to be applied to a concrete set of circumstances."[2] Justice Slatter of the Alberta Court of Appeal put it more colourfully several years back in stating that the "exact content of the duty to consult is in its formative stages, and is still being hammered

---

1 *Haida Nation* v. *British Columbia (Minister of Forests)* [2004] 3 S.C.R. 511, 2004 SCC 73 at para. 11.

2 *Carrier Sekani Tribal Council* v. *British Columbia (Utilities Commission)*, 2009 BCCA 67 at para. 1, affirmed by *Rio Tinto Alcan Inc.* v. *Carrier Sekani Tribal Council*, 2010 SCC 43, [2010] 2 SCR 650.

out on the anvils of justice."[3] Although these statements are no longer new, they remain true today. Many issues concerning the duty to consult continue to be hammered out in the lower courts. At the same time, there is also a reasonably clear body of doctrine on some central points, which this chapter seeks to set out.

Given the Supreme Court's acknowledgement of the ongoing development of the duty to consult in the lower courts, it is the combination of the judgements of the Supreme Court of Canada together with the decisions of lower courts seeking to work with the duty to consult in more applied contexts that actually defines the legal shape of the duty. These lower court judgements are making many details clearer, but, even today, they continue to be complicating some issues on which disagreement is emerging or on which courts are choosing not to answer particular points. Nonetheless, to come to an understanding of the duty to consult, there is no alternative than to grapple with the case law. My aspiration is to fit the case law as well as possible into a principled framework, seeking to integrate rather than divide. It is important to note that there will be different issues in different provinces, with live Aboriginal title issues being vastly more widespread in British Columbia than elsewhere, and the duty to consult case law thus appearing to develop differently when the differences actually arise from dissimilarities in the underlying factual circumstances. In any case, the effort to integrate the law into more principled frameworks has potential.

This chapter examines, in a sense, the place of the duty to consult within the Canadian legal order, framed in terms of three questions:

1.   When does a duty to consult arise?
2.   Who is involved in consultation?
3.   When are there alternatives to consultation?

2.2 Triggering Test

The following chapter will explore the implications of the case law for the content of the duty to consult in particular circumstances. The duty to consult becomes legally relevant based on certain "triggering conditions."

---

3   *R. v. Lefthand*, 2007 ABCA 206, 77 Alta. L.R. (4th) 203 at para. 37; leave to appeal to S.C.C. refused 385 N.R. 392 (21 Feb. 2008)

These triggering conditions denote a set of threshold requirements that must be met before any duty to consult arises in a particular circumstance. In the absence of these triggering conditions, there is no duty to consult.[4] Although one should not push these analogies too far, the question of whether a duty to consult is triggered parallels that of whether a Charter right is engaged. Before we examine if there has been a breach of a Charter right or the Crown has conducted itself in a manner keeping with its duty to consult, we need to know that a particular fact situation raises the question in the first place. Chief Justice McLachlin offers the leading statement of the test in the *Haida Nation* case:

> When precisely does a duty to consult arise? The foundation of the duty in the Crown's honour and the goal of reconciliation suggest that the duty arises when the Crown has knowledge, real or constructive, of the potential existence of the Aboriginal right or title and contemplates conduct that might adversely affect it.[5]

Justice Binnie clarifies in *Mikisew Cree* that the same principle applies in the context of treaty rights.[6]

After the initial trilogy of cases, the *Rio Tinto* decision is arguably the most significant later duty to consult decision. In it, Chief Justice McLachlin reviews and restates the key case law on the duty to consult. As the first edition of this book did, the Court there breaks down the *Haida Nation* test. Chief Justice McLachlin writes:

> This test can be broken down into three elements: (1) the Crown's knowledge, actual or constructive, of a potential Aboriginal claim or right; (2) contemplated Crown conduct; and (3) the potential that the contemplated conduct may adversely affect an Aboriginal claim or right.[7]

---

4   *Haida Nation, supra* note 1 at paras. 34-37; *Mikisew Cree First Nation* v. *Canada (Minister of Canadian Heritage)*, 2005 SCC 69, [2005] 3 S.C.R. 388 at para. 34.

5   *Haida Nation, ibid.* at para. 35.

6   *Mikisew Cree First Nation, supra* note 4 at para. 34.

7   *Rio Tinto Alcan Inc.* v. *Carrier Sekani Tribal Council*, 2010 SCC 43, [2010] 2 SCR 650, at para. 31.

The duty to consult, then, is triggered based on a knowledge element, a contemplated Crown conduct element, and an adverse effect element. The knowledge element is met when the Crown has actual or constructive knowledge of a potential Aboriginal rights or title claim or of an Aboriginal claim under a treaty. The contemplated Crown conduct element is typically met when the Crown is considering an administrative decision of some kind. The adverse effect element is met when the decision could adversely affect Aboriginal title, an Aboriginal right, or a treaty right, with an implicit requirement that the adverse effect be genuine and not wholly speculative.

2.2(a) Knowledge of the Aboriginal Title, Right, or Treaty Right

In terms of the knowledge element, the test as expressed in *Haida Nation* does not contemplate a duty to consult where the government could not possibly have formed an idea of the claimed right,[8] but the test does contemplate a duty even where there is uncertainty about a claim.[9] According to this test, uncertainty about a claim may affect the scope of the duty to consult in particular circumstances, but it does not fundamentally undermine the existence of the duty.[10]

The concept of actual knowledge of an Aboriginal title claim is the most straightforward scenario in terms of the triggering the duty to consult. Where an Aboriginal title claim has been either filed in court or been claimed in the context of negotiations with government, the Crown will have actual knowledge of it. Constructive knowledge of an Aboriginal title claim is slightly more complicated. Where, for example, certain lands are known or reasonably suspected to have been traditionally occupied by an Aboriginal community, the Crown could be deemed to have constructive knowledge of an Aboriginal title claim in respect of such lands where the nature of the traditional and present occupation are such as to give rise to a viable Aboriginal title claim.[11]

This triggering of the duty to consult will have significant implications in areas of the country with unresolved Aboriginal title issues, particularly

---

8   *Haida Nation, supra* note 1 at para. 36.

9   *Ibid.* at para. 37.

10   *Ibid.*

11   Cf. *Mikisew Cree First Nation, supra* note 4 at para. 25.

in British Columbia. However, given the similarity of Aboriginal reserve land to Aboriginal title land, affirmed by the Supreme Court of Canada in *Osoyoos Indian Band*,[12] one may reasonably infer that possible effects on reserve lands will similarly trigger the duty to consult,[13] extending the implications across the country.

The duty to consult, however, is not triggered only by Aboriginal title claims. The doctrine, as expressed in *Haida Nation*, also refers to the triggering of the duty to consult by Aboriginal rights claims. This triggering has a much broader potential than one confined to the context of title claims. An Aboriginal title claim arises only in the context of identifiable lands under a claim of Aboriginal title. An Aboriginal rights claim arises when an Aboriginal pre-contact practice may continue in the form of a modern-day Aboriginal right.[14]

A basic reading of the Supreme Court of Canada's jurisprudence on the duty to consult would suggest that the duty to consult would be triggered in a wide variety of circumstances where the government was actually or constructively aware of an Aboriginal rights claim that could be adversely affected by its contemplated action. Given the sheer diversity of possible Aboriginal rights claims, this dimension of the test raises some complex issues in terms of the scope of the circumstances in which governments might be considered to have knowledge of a potential Aboriginal rights claim. In some cases that have been litigated on the duty to consult, for example, Aboriginal communities have argued that they should be consulted in respect of any government action affecting some dimension of their claimed scope of Aboriginal self-government.[15] However, there are strong arguments for taking a more attenuated approach than the broad approach on the knowledge element to which the initial Supreme Court of Canada cases seem to have been inclined.

There is a complexity worthy of note here. There can be consultation, and even legal requirements of consultation, that is separate from the duty to consult doctrine, including in certain contexts that go beyond the stan-

---

12 *Osoyoos Indian Band* v. *Oliver (Town)* [2001] 3 S.C.R. 746, 2001 SCC 85 at paras. 41-43.

13 *Haida Nation, supra* note 1 at paras. 35-36; *R.* v. *Marshall; R.* v. *Bernard,* [2005] 2 S.C.R. 220, 2005 SCC 43 at para. 25.

14 See, generally, *R.* v. *Van der Peet,* [1996] 2 S.C.R. 507, 137 D.L.R. (4th) 289.

15 See, for example, *Acadia Band* v. *M.N.R.,* 2008 FCA 119, [2008] C.N.L.R. 17 at paras. 4-5.

dard Aboriginal rights context. For example, in *Simon* v. *Canada (Attorney General)*,[16] the Federal Court adjudicated on claims of an obligation to consult on changes to income assistance to First Nations people living on reserves in Atlantic Canada. In the context of granting an injunction against the change, the Court discussed the possibility of consultation being required not due to the duty to consult but due to procedural fairness requirements within common law doctrines of administrative law. There would not be an impact on an Aboriginal right, however, for purposes of the duty to consult. So, no duty to consult in the sense discussed in the present book would be triggered.

An additional complexity here is that the scope of the duty to consult is dependent on the current state of the law on the scope of the Aboriginal rights that undergird a duty to consult in particular circumstances. The Supreme Court of Canada's initial statement of the Aboriginal rights test in *Van der Peet*[17] has been subject to some important critiques, with the Court later taking some of them into consideration in its tweaking of the *Van der Peet* test in *Sappier and Gray*.[18] Thus, one might think there could be possibilities for the Aboriginal rights test to be subject to modification over time in a process of gradual legal change. Ironically, the addition of the duty to consult to the jurisprudence might actually discourage such change. Any future shift in the test for Aboriginal rights would also shift the duty to consult, and to the extent that any shifts in the Aboriginal rights test became foreseeable, the Crown would implicitly have constructive knowledge of potential Aboriginal rights claims under a modified law even before the law changed. So, any suggestions of anything other than reasonably complete stability in the Aboriginal rights test would open new applications of the duty to consult even before these changes could be debated and subjected to adjudication. The effects of suggestions of instability in the Aboriginal rights test thus become a reason against permitting any perception of possible changes in the law in this area. The development of the duty to consult, then, becomes a factor that may discourage the development of other Aboriginal rights jurisprudence. This obviously raises matters that could be subjected to further discussion, but the most that can be said here is to raise the possibility. It will be interesting to watch what

---

16   *Simon* v. *Canada (Attorney General)*, 2012 FC 387.

17   *Van der Peet, supra* note 14.

18   *R.* v. *Sappier; R.* v. *Gray*, [2006] 2 S.C.R. 686, 2006 SCC 54 at paras. 42-49.

happens in the *Roger William* or *Tsilhqot'in Nation* case,[19] which is the Supreme Court of Canada's first consideration of Aboriginal title in nearly a decade and which as of this writing has been heard and is under reserve.

Finally, Crown knowledge of a treaty right that its conduct may adversely affect also triggers the duty to consult. There seems little potential for argument that the Crown was actually and constructively unaware of a particular treaty rights claim, for the Crown is a treaty rights partner in every instance. As Justice Binnie puts it in *Mikisew Cree*, "[i]n the case of a treaty the Crown, as a party, will always have notice of its contents."[20] However, the claims made under a particular treaty, as well as claims as to the correct interpretation of a treaty, will sometimes be more complex. Although the treaty context will significantly modify the approach to the question of whether a duty to consult is triggered,[21] there will continue to be claims made as to treaty rights that turn out in fact not to engage the duty to consult.[22]

An important distinction must be added at this juncture. The *Mikisew Cree* extension of *Haida Nation* into the treaty rights context was in the context of a historical treaty, one of the numbered treaties dating from the Victorian era. The historical treaties have certain shared characteristics in so far as they tend to be fairly schematic in form and to have been negotiated in a context of unequal bargaining power and of Aboriginal communities without legal representation. However, in the last four decades, since the *James Bay and Northern Quebec Agreement* in 1975, there have been a series of modern treaties developed primarily in the context of comprehensive land claims agreements.[23] These treaties tend to be lengthy, detailed documents, negotiated in meticulous legal language in the context of strong representation on both sides of the treaty process and thus call for a

---

19   *Roger William* v. *British Columbia*, 2012 BCCA 285, leave to appeal to Supreme Court of Canada granted 24 January 2013 and hearing held 7 November 2013. When the decision will be released is, as of this writing, uncertain.

20   *Mikisew Cree First Nation*, *supra* note 4 at para. 34.

21   *Ibid.* at paras. 33-34.

22   *Ibid.* at para. 55.

23   For a history of treaties in Canada, see J.R. Miller, *Compact, Contract, Covenant: Aboriginal Treaty-Making in Canada* (Toronto: University of Toronto Press, 2009). On the numbered treaties specifically, see Robert J. Talbot, *Negotiating the Numbered Treaties: An Intellectual and Political Biography of Alexander Morris* (Saskaton: Purich Publishing, 2009).

different form of interpretation and application.[24]

In the duty to consult context in particular, the modern treaties will typically contain consultation clauses where there is negotiated agreement to the need for consultation and concerning modes of consultation in a variety of specified contexts. The result is that the treaty itself becomes the primary referent in determining consultation obligations. Justice Binnie explains the point well in his 2010 majority judgement in *Beckman* v. *Little Salmon/Carmacks First Nation*:

> When a modern treaty has been concluded, the first step is to look at its provisions and try to determine the parties' respective obligations, and whether there is some form of consultation provided for in the treaty itself. If a process of consultation has been established in the treaty, the scope of the duty to consult will be shaped by its provisions.[25]

Where the treaty leaves room for differences of interpretation, the constitutional duty to consult can continue to operate,[26] but the text of a modern treaty will generally take priority in defining consultation obligations in that treaty context. The result is that it will more often be the case that no constitutional duty to consult is triggered. That said, of course, consultation obligations under the treaty will be triggered in accordance with the treaty terms.

In an even more complicated context, there have been disputes about whether a sale of Crown land that could theoretically be purchased with treaty land entitlement (TLE) funds triggers the duty to consult. This question is of major significance in provinces with outstanding TLE entitlements, such as Manitoba and Saskatchewan. There is no specific treaty right, of course, for a First Nation with TLE funds to buy any particular piece of land. However, if the Crown could simply sell each piece of land bit by bit without offering them to communities with TLE funds, the TLE funds could be rendered effectively useless. This issue has been subject to

---

24　See generally, however, Dwight Newman, "Contractual and Covenantal Conceptions of Modern Treaty Making" (2011) 54 S.C.L.R. (2d) 475 (arguing that even the modern treaties still need to be considered as partly covenantal).

25　*Beckman* v. *Little Salmon/Carmacks First Nation*, 2010 SCC 53, [2010] 3 S.C.R. 103, at para. 67.

26　*Ibid.* at paras. 62, 69.

prolonged litigation in a case concerning federal military lands in Winnipeg known as the Kapyong Barracks. Several First Nations had expressed an interest in acquiring the land in order to establish an urban reserve. However, the federal government had taken the view it could transfer the lands for sale to the Canada Lands Company without consultation. Following decisions up and down the appeal chain of courts since 2009, the latest decision of the Federal Court has been that Canada owed and breached a duty to consult in taking the steps to transfer the lands, and the Federal Court granted an injunction against the transfer until meaningful consultation could be shown to have taken place.[27] The Federal Court of Appeal heard an appeal of this decision in December 2013, with that judgement under reserve as of this writing, and its decision will be significant in terms of in what situations a treaty land entitlement-based right does or does not give rise to consultation.

Putting aside these more specific questions and returning to the central principles, in general terms, the test for the triggering of the duty to consult offered in *Haida Nation* contemplates a duty even in the face of significant uncertainty about a particular Aboriginal title or Aboriginal rights claim. As described by McLachlin C.J.C.,

> There is a distinction between knowledge sufficient to trigger a duty to consult and, if appropriate, accommodate, and the content or scope of the duty in a particular case. Knowledge of a credible but unproven claim suffices to trigger a duty to consult and accommodate. The content of the duty, however, varies with the circumstances, as discussed more fully below. A dubious or peripheral claim may attract a mere duty of notice, while a stronger claim may attract more stringent duties. The law is capable of differentiating between tenuous claims, claims possessing a strong prima facie case, and established claims. Parties can assess these matters, and if they cannot agree, tribunals and courts can assist. Difficulties associated with the absence of proof and definition of claims are addressed by assigning appropriate content to the duty, not by denying the existence of a duty.[28]

---

27   *Long Plain First Nation* v. *Canada*, 2012 FC 1474.

28   *Haida Nation, supra* note 1 at para. 37.

Justice Binnie implicitly adopts the same statement for the treaty context in *Mikisew Cree*.[29] In all the different contexts, then, the Supreme Court appears to commend an approach to the knowledge element in the triggering of the duty to consult that considers the duty relatively easily triggered, with adjustment for the relative strength or weakness of the elements underpinning the duty in particular circumstances playing out in the content of the duty in those circumstances.

Lower courts engaged with duty to consult situations since the Supreme Court's early pronouncements have been more ready to add internal limits to the circumstances in which the duty is triggered, thus offering a somewhat more tempered version of the law on the duty to consult. In the context of the knowledge requirement, lower courts have recognized more possibility of a lack of evidence for an Aboriginal title or right to give rise to a non-triggering of the duty to consult. In *Native Council of Nova Scotia v. Canada*,[30] the Federal Court of Canada, in a judgement affirmed on the same grounds by the Federal Court of Appeal,[31] held that the offering of limited evidence to the Court of a claimed Aboriginal right meant that the duty to consult was not engaged. Similarly, in *Ahousaht Indian Band v. Canada (Minister of Fisheries & Oceans)*,[32] the Federal Court of Appeal emphasized that the proof submitted of an Aboriginal right giving rise to consultation requirements needed to go beyond "mere submissions" to meaningful evidence.[33] That said, courts have recognized that it would not be reasonable to demand more than a "credible claim."[34] As a result, where the government could meaningfully form an idea of there being Aboriginal title, an Aboriginal right, or a treaty right, this element of the test will be satisfied.

---

29 *Mikisew Cree, supra* note 4 at para. 33.

30 *Native Council of Nova Scotia* v. *Canada*, 2007 FC 45, [2007] 2 C.N.L.R. 233, 71 Admin. L.R. (4th) 1 at paras. 68-70.

31 *Native Council of Nova Scotia* v. *Canada*, 2008 FCA 113, 165 A.C.W.S. (3d) 1, [2008] 3 C.N.L.R. 286 at para. 5.

32 *Ahousaht Indian Band* v. *Canada (Minister of Fisheries & Oceans)*, 2008 FCA 212, 297 D.L.R. (4th) 722.

33 *Ibid.* at paras. 36-37. See also *Acadia Band* v. *Canada* (M.N.R.), *supra* note 15 at para. 10.

34 See *Labrador Métis Nation* v. *Newfoundland and Labrador (Minister of Transportation and Works)*, 2006 FCA 393 at paras. 43-45, citing *Haida Nation*'s reference at *supra* note 1, paras. 37-38 to a "preliminary evidence-based assessment of the strength of the claim."

2.2(b) Adverse Effect Element of the Triggering Test

Knowledge of the existence of Aboriginal title claims, Aboriginal rights claims, and treaty rights claims grounds the duty to consult in general terms. However, for there to be a duty to consult in particular circumstances, the knowledge of a particular title or rights claim must be linked to the contemplation of government action that, on the Supreme Court of Canada's description, "might adversely affect it."[35] Although this phrase did not appear to call for an especially stringent test but similarly for a reasonably easy triggering of a duty to consult, it has nonetheless given rise in lower courts' jurisprudence to some internal limits on when the duty to consult is triggered. The Supreme Court of Canada has now arguably embraced this view, with the Court in *Rio Tinto* concluding that it is actually necessary to have the "demonstration of a causal connection between the proposed Crown conduct and a potential adverse impact on an Aboriginal claim or right."[36] That said, even at the very same time in the very same case, McLachlin C.J.C. has continued to insist on a generous approach to this part of the test:

> Again, a generous, purposive approach to this element is in order, given that the doctrine's purpose, as stated by Newman, is "to recognize that actions affecting unproven Aboriginal title or rights or treaty rights can have irreversible effects that are not in keeping with the honour of the Crown" (p. 30, citing *Haida Nation*, at paras. 27 and 33). Mere speculative impacts, however, will not suffice. As stated in *R. v. Douglas*, 2007 BCCA 265, 278 D.L.R. (4th) 653, at para. 44, there must an "appreciable adverse effect on the First Nations' ability to exercise their aboriginal right." The adverse effect must be on the future exercise of the right itself; an adverse effect on a First Nation's future negotiating position does not suffice.[37]

The fact that there would be internal limits is appropriate. The Supreme Court's original terminology concerning the duty reflects a view of there being some limits on the effects considered to give rise to a duty to consult, for it requires not just any effect but a specifically detrimental effect, giv-

---

35   *Haida Nation, supra* note 1 at para. 35.

36   *Rio Tinto, supra* note 7 at para. 51.

37   *Ibid.* at para. 46.

ing scope for evaluating the effects in a particular instance. Corresponding to this, some of the suggested internal limits propose that the duty to consult not be triggered where there is a relatively minimal adverse effect. For example, the British Columbia Court of Appeal in *Douglas*[38] held that a duty to consult was not triggered by a policy change that had "no appreciable adverse effect on the First Nations' ability to exercise their Aboriginal right."[39] This case was in the context of a limitation on an established right — specifically, whether the development of certain rules on a sport fishery required further consultation after there had been consultation with Aboriginal communities about an overall fisheries strategy — with the Court deciding that the consultation about the overall strategy was adequate without further discussion. The case nonetheless helps us interpret the triggering standard. The Court cited this "no appreciable effect" standard back to *Haida Nation*'s test on adverse effect,[40] although it obviously adds a gloss to the test in that it begins to suggest that one can look to how "appreciable" any adverse effect is.

The Alberta Court of Appeal in *Lefthand* would seemingly have imposed even more substantial limits.[41] Slatter J. A.'s judgement would recognize a duty to consult only where a *prima facie* breach of an Aboriginal or treaty right was established,[42] and would recognize a *prima facie* breach only where the accused could show some "unreasonableness, hardship, or interference" resulting in a preferred means of exercising the right.[43] Other judgements in the case, notably that of Conrad J. A., appear in some respects to be going back to pre-*Haida Nation* in their analysis, so the case may not fully reflect an interpretation of the modern duty. But it nonetheless suggests the view of some appellate courts that there needs to be a larger set of internal limits on the triggering test for a duty to consult.

In the absence of appropriate internal limits, the government actions potentially subject to consultation obligations would become virtually boundless. A recent Federal Court decision in *Hupacasath First Nation* v.

38 *R.* v. *Douglas*, 2007 BCCA 265, 278 D.L.R. (4th) 263; leave to appeal to S.C.C. refused 383 N.R. 382 (15 Nov. 2007).

39 *Ibid.* at para. 44.

40 *Ibid.*

41 *Lefthand, supra* note 3.

42 *Ibid.* at para. 38.

43 *Ibid.* at para. 126.

Canada (Minister of Foreign Affairs)[44] illustrates the point. The case concerned whether Canada had a duty to consult the Hupacasath First Nation prior to signing a foreign investment agreement with China. The Hupacasath First Nation tried to argue that there might be some circumstance in which the agreement led Canada to be less respectful of certain Aboriginal rights. The judge ultimately held such impacts to be speculative and nonappreciable, rejecting in the process tendered expert evidence that made a variety of complaints about such foreign investment agreements. Such a ruling seems quite correct. Vague allegations of connections between some action and some highly speculative effect in respect of Aboriginal rights ought not to trigger consultation obligations in advance of major foreign policy initiatives. It is important to have a line concerning speculative impacts, or the duty to consult becomes an inappropriate and undue hindrance to government action that is entirely unproblematic vis-à-vis Aboriginal interests.

Perhaps trickier are situations involving different types of reorganization of governance structures. A particularly prominent case of this sort was *Adams Lake Indian Band* v. *British Columbia (Lieutenant Governor in Council)*.[45] This case concerned claims by the Aboriginal community that there was a duty to consult applicable prior to the incorporation of a municipality in its traditional territories, specifically in circumstances where the municipality was being organized so as to further certain kinds of resort development. The British Columbia Court of Appeal held, however, that there was no inherent connection between incorporation of the municipality and any effect on Aboriginal rights, and the Supreme Court of Canada denied leave to appeal this decision. Situations involving a reorganization of governance will arguably not typically trigger a duty to consult, since the question is ultimately what the new governing structure chooses to do.

The Supreme Court's stated purpose in *Haida Nation* was to recognize that actions affecting unproven Aboriginal title or rights or treaty rights can have irreversible effects that are not in keeping with the honour of the Crown.[46] To the extent that case law in lower courts goes too far in setting new standards of proof of *prima facie* breaches, it is inconsistent with the

---

44   *Hupacasath First Nation* v. *Canada (Minister of Foreign Affairs)*, 2013 FC 900.

45   *Adams Lake Indian Band* v. *British Columbia (Lieutenant Governor in Council)*, 2012 BCCA 333, leave to appeal denied 11 April 2013.

46   *Haida Nation, supra* note 1 at paras. 27, 33

main thrust of the *Haida Nation* jurisprudence. To the extent that lower court case law recognizes that there needs to be a real adverse effect at issue before a duty to consult is triggered, however, it carries forward the duty to consult test. Although the Supreme Court seemingly offered an easily triggered duty, with scope for modification of the requirements in a specific context, the triggering of a duty to consult by every government action that could, through some remote process, have some minimal adverse effect on an Aboriginal right would set up an impractical scenario for government decision-making. To say this much is not to undermine the purposes of the duty to consult, but to make it workable and efficacious in furthering reconciliation processes. It is also appropriate to conclude, as the Federal Court of Appeal has, that a situation where a government action might affect an Aboriginal right, but only through a remote causal chain, does not trigger a duty to consult.[47]

The precise triggering test may depend on the sort of right at issue. There are powerful arguments in the lower court case law that the reason for an apparently easy triggering test in the early Supreme Court of Canada cases was partly motivated by the context of Aboriginal title that could be irreversibly affected. Where one is concerned with an Aboriginal right in which the government action could be reversed without lasting effect on that right, there is surely a stronger argument for a constitutional duty to consult not being triggered as readily.

One particularly significant implication of the adverse impact requirement concerns historic impacts on Aboriginal rights. Fully historic impacts do not trigger a duty to consult because the duty to consult is proactive and forward-looking and not geared to trying to solve every problem of the past. This was a fundamental conclusion in the *Rio Tinto* case. There, McLachlin C.J.C. made this implication explicit:

> The third element of a duty to consult is the possibility that the Crown conduct may affect the Aboriginal claim or right. The claimant must show a causal relationship between the proposed government conduct or decision and a potential for adverse impacts on pending Aboriginal claims or rights. Past wrongs, including previous breaches of the duty to consult, do not suffice.[48]

---

47   *Labrador Métis Nation, supra* note 34 at paras. 4, 29, 227.

48   *Rio Tinto, supra* note 7 at para. 45.

The facts of the case concerned the British Columbia Utilities Commission's approval of a renewal of energy purchase agreements for energy from a dam built decades ago without consultation at the time. The renewal of these agreements would have no new impact, so it did not trigger a duty to consult. Similar conclusions have properly followed in other cases concerning renewals of permits, such as in the Federal Court of Appeal's decision in the context of the renewal of an operating licence for a northern Saskatchewan uranium mine in *Fond du Lac Denesuline First Nation* v. *Canada (Attorney General).*[49]

However, a different Federal Court decision reached a very different conclusion on this point. In *Kwicksutaineuk Ah-Kwa-Mish First Nation* v. *Canada (Attorney General)*, de Montigny J. reasoned as follows:

> For the duty to be triggered, there must be a new decision or conduct that may affect Aboriginal rights. The re-issuance of a licence, even if it is similar to the one it is replacing, is certainly sufficient to meet the third requirement underlying the duty to consult (see, for example, *Upper Nicola Indian Band* v *British Columbia (Minister of Environment)*, 2011 BCSC 388 at paras 103-114, 21 BCLR (5th) 81). It is a fresh action, so much so that in the absence of the renewed licence, the commercial activity authorized by that licence would have to come to a halt. In my view, the duty to consult arises each time a licence is renewed, because each new licence may potentially affect the claim right or title, if only incrementally. Otherwise, the duty to consult would be spent once the initial licence has been granted, for however long a period it is renewed and irrespective of the impacts the renewed licences may have down the road. Such a reasoning would make a mockery of the duty to consult and of the honour of the Crown.[50]

With respect, this reasoning, while having some logic to it, appears to be inconsistent with the main conclusion from *Rio Tinto* and the Federal Court of Appeal's application of that principle to a licence renewal in *Fond*

---

49 *Fond du Lac Denesuline First Nation* v. *Canada (Attorney General)*, 2012 FCA 73.

50 *Kwicksutaineuk Ah-Kwa-Mish First Nation* v. *Canada (Attorney General)*, 2012 FC 517 at para. 110.

du Lac Denesuline First Nation v. *Canada (Attorney General)*.[51] The statement of de Montigny J., while reflecting ongoing debate within the law, probably does not reflect good law on this point.

A variant on the question of historic breaches may arise in the context of cases where a historical background of past wrongs somehow bears on the forward-looking effects of a present decision, and *West Moberly,* a major British Columbia Court of Appeal case in 2011, actually suggested that it would be appropriate to make reference to historic breaches as part of how to understand a present decision's effects where historic breaches and present decisions together had any kind of cumulative effect.[52] The situations to which this decision applies are not wholly clear and may need further development in the jurisprudence before they can be properly interpreted. Past impacts were considered not relevant in the *Louis* case, where the British Columbia Court of Appeal in 2013 even held that a minor expansion of a mine size did not constitute a new impact and thus did not properly trigger a duty to consult.[53] The fundamental point that the concern of the duty to consult is with genuine forward-looking impacts from present government decisions seems to stand as the main take-away from the case law thus far. The Supreme Court of Canada's recent refusal of leave to appeal the *Louis* case arguably reinforces this point and emphasizes that the courts are limiting the duty to consult where Aboriginal groups are trying to use past alleged infringements, have overlapping claims, or do not cooperate in the duty to consult process.[54]

This conclusion in respect of historic breaches has some interesting implications. One important implication in the context of certain kinds

---

51 *Fond du Lac Denesuline First Nation, supra* note 49.

52 *West Moberly First Nations* v. *British Columbia (Chief Inspector of Mines)*, 2011 BCCA 247, leave to appeal to Supreme Court of Canada refused 23 February 2012.

53 *Louis* v. *British Columbia (Minister of Energy, Mines, and Petroleum Resources)*, 2013 BCCA 412, leave to appeal to Supreme Court of Canada refused 27 February 2014.

54 See discussion of the Court of Appeal decision in *Louis* in Kevin O'Callaghan & Jonathan Conlin, "Aboriginal consultation for BC mine expansion upheld," Fasken Martineau Aboriginal Law Bulletin (August 25, 2011), available online http://www.fasken.com/files/Publication/ad5f0feb-6899-4958-9458-08ed970e3a14/Presentation/PublicationAttachment/b94b737c-8dc4-45b5-8fb4-b077afa97d1a/Aboriginal%20Law%20Bulletin%20August%2025%20EN.pdf

of resource transportation developments, such as pipelines, is that use or construction along any kind of existing right of way will be legally much simpler than attempting to gain approval for any new right of way. This difference is not, of course, unique to the duty to consult context, for new rights of way will always give rise to issues. But, in other areas of the law, there are solutions like compensated expropriation. In the duty to consult context, the sheer legal challenges of dealing with the duty to consult along the route of a new pipeline that crosses many traditional territories, and the delays that may ensue, may pose a real challenge for potential investors. Holdout communities may exert large degrees of pressure, more so than in other legal contexts, so the duty to consult has a particularly strong force in generating differences between existing routes and new rights of way.

That said, the same principles about historic breaches undergird another important conclusion, which is that limitation periods apply to duty to consult claims. Attempts to challenge decisions of some time ago based on the duty to consult will be subject to standard limitation periods that time bar claims.[55] Again, the duty to consult is focused on future adverse effects and is not a means of dealing with speculative harms or past harms. However, even in that differentiation, it may pose some real challenges in certain policy contexts.

2.2 (c) Contemplated Government Conduct

The test's remaining element concerning contemplated government conduct, which may initially appear straightforward, can actually be a further complicating factor. The Supreme Court of Canada's case law does not delve meaningfully into an analysis of what level of contemplation is needed for particular government planning to trigger the duty to consult. In some situations, in which the duty to consult has significant relevance, the issue requires more detailed analysis. For example, if the government issues a permit for exploratory steps that might move toward a larger project, but only if it turns out to be economically worthwhile, the question is whether the granting of a permit at the initial stage triggers the duty to consult, or if the duty to consult is triggered only in consideration of the larger project. There is something to think about in this area largely because the Federal

---

55 See *Athabasca Chipewyan First Nation* v. *Alberta (Minister of Energy)*, 2011 ABCA 29, leave to appeal to Supreme Court of Canada refused 23 February 2012.

Court in a 2007 decision in *Dene Tha' First Nation* v. *Canada*[56] took a view of contemplated conduct that looks to a larger project that could reasonably be seen to flow from the current decision-making processes. In the case, Phelan J. adopted this approach in the context of early decisions related to the construction of the MacKenzie Gas Pipeline, noting that the pipeline was not merely an idea in the heads of a few governmental officials but a plan with a road map toward the project,[57] and holding that this meant there should have been consultation from that earlier stage. The factual element of there being a definite longer-term plan present might make the case unique on its facts. But Phelan J.'s reasoning does seem to lend itself to a broader reading of the principle here. Justice Phelan cites back to what was really at stake with the tree farm licenses in *Haida Nation*,[58] arguing that the conduct contemplated in granting a tree farm license properly engaged the duty to consult not so much because of the specific license decision but because it involved "strategic planning for the utilization of the resource."[59]

At a very practical level, Saskatchewan's system for mineral, oil, and gas dispositions provides an interesting example that might weigh in the other direction.[60] For mineral rights, Saskatchewan's system continues to be based on staking — physical staking in the north and map-staking in the south — with the party staking and filing a claim with the Ministry of Energy and Resources gaining legal priority over all others in the rights to the minerals.[61] For oil and gas rights, a company confidentially requests that rights in a certain area be put for sale and the Province then puts them up for sale at quarterly auctions. The Ministry is now putting caveats in

---

56 *Dene Tha' First Nation* v. *Canada (Minister of Environment)*, 2006 FC 1354, [2007] 1 C.N.L.R. 1 [*Dene Tha' (Fed. Ct.)*], aff'd 2008 FCA 20, 378 N.R. 251.

57 *Ibid.* at para. 100.

58 *Ibid.* at para. 106.

59 *Ibid.* at para. 106, citing *Haida Nation*, *supra* note 1 at para. 76.

60 I am indebted to Mitch McAdam for drawing this issue to my attention. He discussed the issue in a Saskatchewan Legal Education Society presentation, "Duty to Consult and Accommodate Aboriginal and Treaty Rights: A Practical Guide for Legal Practitioners Involved in the Mining, Oil and Gas Industries" (30 Sept. 2008).

61 The system is elaborated in *Crown Minerals Act,* S.S. 1984-85-86, c. C-50.2; *Mineral Resources Act*, 1985, S.S. 1984-85-86, c. M-16.1; and *Mineral Disposition Regulations*, 1996, Sask. Reg. 30/86.

some land sale notices to alert prospective purchasers that duty to consult requirements may arise in the development of certain lands.[62] The Ministry has also taken the position that it can carry out the sale of oil and gas rights without consultation at that stage. It says this is because Aboriginal interests would not be affected until there is an actual permit to develop those oil and gas rights — that then being the stage at which duty to consult requirements would arise — and there is now some judicial support for this position.[63] Although Aboriginal communities have challenged this position, it does have a degree of significant practicality to it. Until an actual decision is under contemplation that has the potential to affect rights, the sale of oil and gas rights that might or might not be developed — depending on later decisions on various other issues — and that might be developed in a variety of ways, each having potentially different implications for Aboriginal interests, arguably cannot be considered to trigger the duty to consult with every Aboriginal community that might be affected in some future scenario after the issuance of further permits.

However, thinking of the duty to consult in a permit-by-permit manner is arguably inconsistent with the reasoning in the *Dene Tha'* case, and there is a possibility that such an approach could result in "death by a thousand cuts."[64] If an Aboriginal community does not realize the significance of each permit being issued as part of a larger project, it may not have a fair opportunity to respond to the effect of the overall project. Indeed, a permit-by-permit approach to consultation may be impractical and unworkable for all concerned,[65] since it will set in motion a process for each permit in a manner inconsistent with the goals of the duty to consult and creating delays and problems in the meantime.

---

62 See the *Petroleum and Natural Gas Regulations*, 1969, Sask. Reg. 8/69, s. 43.5.g.i.

63 McAdam discusses this position, *supra* note 60. It appears to have carried the day in a recent decision of the Saskatchewan Court of Queen's Bench in a case concerning the Buffalo River Dene released on March 11, 2014: *Buffalo River Dene Nation* v. *Ministry of Energy and Resources*, 2014 SCQB 69.

64 I am grateful to my former colleague, the emeritus law professor Marie-Ann Bowden, for discussions on this point.

65 Cf. "Seeking Common Ground: Roundtable Conference on First Nations and Métis Consultation and Accommodation: Conference Report" (Regina: Government of Saskatchewan Ministry of First Nations and Métis Relations, 2008): www.fnmr.gov.sk.ca/roundtable-conference-report.

That said, there need not be consultation about every broader choice. In *Halalt First Nation*, a modified permit developed in response to accommodation after initial consultation involved fewer wells from an aquifer but also involved year-round pumping.[66] The British Columbia Court of Appeal held that there was not an obligation to consult newly on the adjustment to year-round pumping and specifically rejected the trial judge's application of the "death by a thousand cuts" analogy on the particular facts of the case.[67]

In some circumstances, it may be appropriate for the government to consult on a general strategy such that the duty to consult would not then be engaged by every decision along the way.[68] However, these matters must be decided in the manner most appropriate to the issues at stake. As part of its approach to consultation in particular circumstances, the government ought to consider in good faith whether a particular decision is inherently connected to a larger strategy or project in a manner other than exploring the possibility of that strategy or project. If so, it may be appropriate to consider consultation about the larger undertaking from the outset, or at least from whenever it crystallizes.

The Supreme Court of Canada has now adopted this basic principle. Although it did not need to affirm the point in light of the matters at issue in the case, in *Rio Tinto* the Court ended up adopting the position that "government action is not confined to decisions or conduct which have an immediate impact on lands and resources. A potential for adverse impact suffices. Thus, the duty to consult extends to 'strategic, higher level decisions' that may have an impact on Aboriginal claims and rights."[69] This statement, however, is pregnant with possible implications, to which fuller attention follows below. For the moment, it is worth simply noting that the scope of contemplated government conduct may be larger than the specific decision at issue, depending on what analysis is most appropriate in all of the circumstances.

---

66 *Halalt First Nation* v. *British Columbia (Minister of the Environment)*, 2012 BCCA 472, leave to appeal refused 18 January 2013.

67 *Ibid.* at paras. 88, 134-38.

68 *Lefthand, supra* note 3 at para. 40, per Slatter J. A.

69 *Rio Tinto, supra* note 7, at para. 44.

2.2(d) Summary on Triggering Test and Implications

The application of the triggering test is obviously far from simple. Where government departments are uncertain about whether their action triggers a duty to consult, the safer course may be to act as if it did and extend at least notice of the proposed action to potentially affected Aboriginal communities. After all, a failure to consult may provoke litigation that will cause delays in the government action. Moreover, there is an important rationale for some ease in the triggering of a duty to consult; in circumstances where an Aboriginal community will be able to add to the Crown understanding of the extent of impact of particular decisions, it may be valuable for the duty to be considered triggered simply in order to ensure that there is input from the Aboriginal community.

Government departments need not consult in circumstances where there are major doubts about the Aboriginal title or right or treaty right. They need not consult in circumstances where there is no plausible adverse effect on an Aboriginal claim. They need not consult if they are not involved in the kinds of action that trigger a duty to consult. However, it is not always easy for government officials to make those determinations with certainty, which may support the notion that to avoid the risk of not consulting in circumstances where consultation should have occurred, where there is any argument for doing so and it is practical to do so, notice to Aboriginal communities should at least be extended. Indeed, given the ease with which the duty to consult may be triggered, it will sometimes be a wise move for governments to engage in consultation even while maintaining the position that they are not legally required to do so. In *Kʼomoks First Nation* v. *Canada (Attorney General)*,[70] the federal Minister had followed such a course of action in the context of reissuing fish farm licences within a community's traditional territory. Because of this, there could be no duty to consult claim made because consultation had already occurred. However, it would be impractical to consult on every governmental decision; there is a need for good judgement in applying this principle of consulting where there is plausible reason to think that consultation may be required.

There may be other exceptions to the standard triggering test as well. For example, there are judicial statements to the effect that, if urgent circumstances preclude consultation in a particular instance, this may mean

---

70   *Kʼomoks First Nation* v. *Canada*, 2012 FC 1160, 419 FTR 144.

that a duty to consult is not triggered.[71] Similarly, in a case concerning the decision of a prosecutor to go ahead with a case, the Federal Court of Appeal has suggested that the principles of the separation of powers mean that the prosecutor is not under a duty to consult.[72] Thus, there may be exceptions to the duty to consult in light of emergency needs or other vital interests. Although any broad reading of such an exception would vitiate the purposes of the doctrine, any decision not to have such an exception would undermine the aims of the law as well. Thus, there may be additional exceptions in special circumstances, as guided by the purposes of the duty to consult doctrine.

2.3 Role of Early Engagement

Because of the relative ease with which the duty to consult is triggered, one implication is the significant value of early engagement. Three key reasons make early engagement valuable, each in different ways. First, putting aside the law and concentrating on the relationships that the duty to consult seeks to foster, early engagement with communities can help build trust and relationships prior to rushed decision-making stages. Second, from a legal standpoint, there will be times when early engagement is effectively mandatory. Where a decision falls within the concept of a strategic decision that determines later decisions — an idea fleshed out further elsewhere in this chapter — it will be legally mandatory to engage early concerning that decision and thus to enter into early engagement with the Aboriginal community, prior to the consideration of more specific decisions that arise within the scope of the broader strategic decision. And, third, early engagement may well serve as an important legal shield against challenges concerning lack of consultation.

On this last point, where some kind of reasonable consultation process is underway, the courts are unlikely to entertain a legal challenge during that process but would rather prefer that the process unfold before there is a challenge.[73] A rights claim that may arise in future does not generally

---

71   *Lefthand, supra* note 3, at para 45.

72   *Ibid.* at paras. 24, 29. See also *Ochapowace First Nation (Indian Band No. 71) v. Canada (Attorney General)*, 2009 FCA 124 at para. 37, suggesting that the exercise of police discretion is also in a realm outside the application of the duty to consult.

73   *Gitxaala Nation v. Canada (Minister of Transport, Infrastructure, and Com-*

justify litigation now.[74] The courts do not want to adjudicate on duty to consult processes in the abstract but only if there remains a dispute after consultation.[75] The role of the courts, rather, is try to foster good faith, meaningful consultation. Where that is occurring or has occurred, it will be an extra reason for the courts to intervene in ways supportive of that process, such as through granting orders against blockades that seek to turn to some other means of dispute resolution.[76] Early engagement may well be a sign of good faith efforts at meaningful consultation, and those pursuing meaningful consultation will wish to consider carefully how early they can enter into consultation to make it as fully meaningful as possible.

Broadly speaking, it is important to have a record of consultation, and even early engagement may become part of that record unless specifically conducted on a "non-consultation" basis. Early engagement, in addition, may well form part of meaningful consultation. The government's assessment of the depth of consultation required is sometimes reviewed with no allowance for error.[77] However, more generally, the courts have in a number of cases indicated that the matter under examination in a challenge asserting a lack of fulfillment of the duty to consult is the reasonableness of the government action in the circumstances.[78] The courts will not seek to intervene simply because there has been some imperfection in the process; they are concerned with whether there has been a reasonable effort at consultation and, where appropriate, accommodation.[79] Have the Crown's actions been "within a range of reasonably defensible approaches"?[80] The

---

munities), 2012 FC 1336, 421 F.T.R. 169.

74   *Campbell* v. *British Columbia (Minister of Forests and Range)*, 2012 BCCA 468, [2013] 1 C.N.L.R. 10.

75   *Cold Lake First Nations* v. *Alberta (Energy Resources Conservation Board)*, 2012 ABCA 304.

76   *Nalcor Energy* v. *Nunatukavut Community Council*, 2012 NLTD(G) 175, 330 Nfld. & P.E.I.R. 233.

77   *White River First Nation* v. *Yukon (Minister of Energy, Mines, and Resources)*, 2013 YKSC 66.

78   See, for example, *Native Council of Nova Scotia*, *supra* note 31 at para. 89; *Labrador Métis Nation*, *supra* note 34 at para. 52; *Lefthand*, *supra* note 3 at para. 42.

79   *Haida Nation*, *supra* note 1 at para. 62 and 63.

80   *Ke-Kin-is-Uqs* v. *British Columbia (Minister of Forests)*, 2008 BCSC 1505, [2009] 1 C.N.L.R. 30 at para. 252. .

standard in this area, according to several courts touching on the matter, has not been altered by recent major developments in administrative law generally.[81] But if the Crown has misconceived what is required of it, particularly by incorrectly concluding that a duty to consult is at a lower end of the spectrum than it is, then this may render its process unreasonable.[82] Thus, the courts show a meaningful degree of deference to the development of reasonable processes and do not seek to intervene in every instance, but they do stand ready to intervene in an instance where the Crown party has fundamentally failed the duty to consult.

For the government to establish that it has carried out consultation, it must be ready to provide a meaningful record to the courts. In a case involving the Hupacasath First Nation,[83] the British Columbia Supreme Court considered a 1663-page "consultation record" supplied by government lawyers. Much of it consisted of draft meeting notes rather than minutes and much of it contained specialized terminology not understandable to an outside reader; the Court concluded that the record did not "speak for itself."[84] To ensure that issues can be resolved effectively in the case of disputes arising over the process in a duty to consult, it is important for all stakeholders to keep detailed records of discussions and consultations that have taken place. Because it is a legal doctrine, the duty to consult entails a relatively formal process. Less formal discussions may be valuable in some contexts, but the degree of legal formality that informs the duty to consult obliges parties to think carefully about the effects of entering into informal discussions if there is any later dispute.

2.4 Consultation on Strategic Decisions and Legislation

One of the thornier dimensions of the case law thus far — in the sense of generating a rule that is genuinely difficult to apply — is the suggestion that consultation must legally commence at the point of higher-level or strategic decisions that affect later decisions. The Supreme Court of Canada put the point this way in its decision in *Rio Tinto*: "government action

---

81 *Ahousaht First Nation, supra* note 32 at para. 34; *Tzeachten First Nation* v. *Canada (Attorney General)*, 2007 BCCA 133, 281 D.L.R. (4th) 752, at para. 24.

82 See, for example, *Ke-Kin-is-Uqs, supra* note 80 at paras. 180, 240.

83 *Ibid.*

84 *Ibid.* at paras 42, 50.

is not confined to decisions or conduct which have an immediate impact on lands and resources. A potential for adverse impact suffices. Thus, the duty to consult extends to 'strategic, higher level decisions' that may have an impact on Aboriginal claims and rights."[85] This statement is, of course, right in principle. Where a strategic decision will determine the course of a series of later decisions, avoiding an adverse impact on Aboriginal or treaty rights may very plausibly be better achieved by consulting at the strategic stage.

However, what this means in practice is much more challenging. Governments may need to have the room to approach consultation at this earlier stage in a more flexible manner that does not necessarily involve the same kind of consultation with each individual Aboriginal community. Many strategic decisions about larger policy choices will have a much larger ambit of impact. It would not be unreasonable, then, to have some kind of consultation that occurs in a different way that does leave room for input from the Aboriginal community generally but that does not necessarily seek to alter the policy in response to a series of quite possibly competing arguments put by different Aboriginal communities that might be affected in different ways and more or less supportive of a particular policy choice.

One ideal approach might be consultation with a body delegated for such consultations by individual rights-bearing communities. If Aboriginal communities do not organize themselves in that way, however, governments may wish to contemplate simply some kind of public consultation process with a special place for Aboriginal participation and/or some kind of Aboriginal participation within the decision-making body itself. The duty to consult doctrine should leave room for this kind of modified approach in the context of the genuinely challenging problem of consultation at the strategic stage of larger decisions.

The challenges associated with the suggestion that the duty to consult applies at the more formative stages of policies become even more accentuated when one starts thinking about something like legislative activity. Whether the creation of legislation is subject to the application of the constitutional duty to consult has been debated over time.[86] The first position

---

85   *Rio Tinto, supra* note 7, at para. 44.

86   The constitutional duty to consult is distinguished here from consultation policy in particular jurisdictions. As will be discussed in Chapter 4, some jurisdictions, like Saskatchewan, have committed to consultation on legislative activity within their duty to consult policies.

on the issue was that expressed in certain judicial decisions on the point in Alberta. According to this Alberta case law, the creation of legislation is outside the application of the duty to consult. This was one of the conclusions of the Alberta Court of Queen's Bench in the *Tsuu T'ina* case,[87] in which it decided that the Minister's recommendation of and Cabinet's adoption of a water management plan had not breached any consultation requirement. The Court there followed what it conceived as one determination of the Alberta Court of Appeal decision in *Lefthand*,[88] in which the Alberta Court of Appeal held that there was no violation of duty to consult requirements in the Alberta government's establishment of a "bait ban." Interpreting the *Lefthand* decision is complicated because the Court split three ways. However, Slatter J. A.'s judgement does put forcefully the claim that legislative processes are not subject to the duty to consult; it would be "an unwarranted interference with the proper functioning of the House of Commons and the Provincial Legislatures to require that they engage in any particular processes prior to the passage of legislation."[89] Watson J. A. concurs,[90] thus making it the majority view of the Alberta Court of Appeal in this case.

However, the *Lefthand* case is certainly not the last word on the point. Indeed, the *Tsuu T'ina* approach was varied within the Alberta courts themselves, as the Alberta Court of Appeal decision in the case suggested, for instance, that the position on legislation might be different than the trial court or the *Lefthand* case had appeared to suggest. As put by O'Brien J.A., "[a]n inability to quash legislation, if that be the case, does not mean that consultation is not required when drafting plans for development of natural resources, nor does it preclude the availability of declaratory relief in appropriate circumstances."[91] Indeed, O'Brien J.A. went on to say: "even if the Legislature itself does not have a duty to consult prior to passing legislation, the duty may still fall upon those assigned the task of developing the policy behind the legislation, or upon those who are charged with making

---

87   *Tsuu T'ina First Nation* v. *Alberta (Environment)* (2008), 96 Alta. L.R. (4th) 65, 2008 ABQB 547 at paras. 57-59 [*Tsuu T'ina trial*]. The decision was affirmed in the result but not on this point in the Court of Appeal in *Tsuu T'ina First Nation* v. *Alberta (Environment)*, 2010 ABCA 137 [*Tsuu T'ina appeal*].

88   *Tsuu T'ina trial, ibid.* at para. 59, citing *Lefthand, supra* note 3.

89   *Lefthand, supra* note 3 at para. 38.

90   *Ibid.* at para. 194.

91   *Tsuu T'ina appeal, supra* note 87, at para. 52.

recommendations concerning future policies and actions."[92] Although the Court of Appeal reached the same conclusion as the trial judge in the case, based on a conclusion that any duty arising had been met, the Court of Appeal judgement in *Tsuu T'ina* effectively suggested that the steps preceding legislative action may well be subject to the duty to consult, even if the legislative process itself is not, which was a significant adjustment from some possible readings of *Lefthand*.

Moreover, apart from the Alberta Court of Appeal's nuancing of its prior position, the Supreme Court of Canada in *Rio Tinto* actually goes out of its way to indicate that the question of the application of the duty to consult to legislative action remains an open question. The Court in no way needed to decide the point but, at the end of a paragraph about the duty to consult on strategic and higher-level decisions, it added the following statement: "We leave for another day the question of whether government conduct includes legislative action: see *R. v. Lefthand*, 2007 ABCA 206, 77 Alta. L.R. (4th) 203, at paras. 37-40."[93] The Court's explicit reference to *Lefthand* combined with the suggestion that the question is for another day suggest that it wishes genuinely to leave the point open.

In the context of the Idle No More movement and the debate about the federal government's omnibus Bill C-45 in 2012,[94] one of the originating issues for the Idle No More movement concerned an alleged lack of consultation on Bill C-45 and a suggestion by that movement that there should have been consultation with Aboriginal communities concerning the possible effects of Bill C-45 on Aboriginal and treaty rights. At the time, some even wrote in support of this in possibly questionable ways. For example, leading Aboriginal law scholar Kent McNeil wrote an op-ed piece in the *Toronto Star* in which he wrote as if it was already legally definitive that there was a constitutional duty to consult on legislative action and therefore there should have been consultation on Bill C-45.[95] Such writing is unhelpful when it presents a point as legally determined when it clearly remains open. The Supreme Court of Canada's explicit signalling of the

---

92   *Ibid.* at para. 56.

93   *Rio Tinto, supra* note 7, at para. 44.

94   Bill C-45 was ultimately passed as the *Jobs and Growth Act, 2012,* S.C. 2012, c. 31 but was long known informally as Bill C-45.

95   Kent McNeil, "Idle No More Deserves Our Thanks," *Toronto Star* (27 January 2013).

point as open for further debate received no mention in McNeil's piece. Some communities did move toward litigation over Bill C-45, and if that litigation proceeds, we may yet see a judicial decision consider the point squarely. But at the moment, much remains indeterminate in the law on this point.

The recent decision in *Ross River Dena Council*,[96] however, does relate to this point in some interesting ways. The Yukon Court of Appeal (drawn from the same pool of judges as the British Columbia Court of Appeal) ended up holding that the duty to consult doctrine meant that Yukon had to modify its mining legislation. Its long-standing "free entry" mining legislation permitted some staking activity that then resulted in an automatic permit for certain activities, with no statutory discretion on whether to issue the permit. No consultation would take place because there was no administrative decision being made but simply an issuance of a permit to which the prospector was legally entitled. The Court held that this approach did not make room for consultation and thus required amendments to be made to the legislation to make room for consultation. The Supreme Court of Canada recently denied leave to appeal from this decision. It may be that the Supreme Court wishes simply more time to consider the issue and more appellate pronouncements. But the effect in the meantime is that the duty to consult has been allowed to become a doctrine under which legislation can be declared unconstitutional. It is no longer a doctrine simply about decisions made by government officials, but it has in some ways become something by which legislation can be evaluated. It would be logically consistent with this position that a duty to consult would apply to legislative action, but the point actually goes even farther to significantly change the application of the doctrine.

This shift in the doctrine may well not be positive. If the doctrine is about the establishment of a duty of consultation on governments to consider the effects of their actions on Aboriginal communities in a proactive way by consulting with those communities, that likely supports reconciliation. If the doctrine begins to become a means by which various pieces of government legislation are struck down, it is likely to awaken concerns about a form of judicial activism in a manner that may well not further reconciliation.

More generally, although there are some good reasons that do support the application of the duty to legislative action, there are sound reasons

96   *Ross River Dena Council* v. *Government of Yukon*, 2012 YKCA 14, leave to appeal refused 19 September 2013.

to worry about that application as well. Notably, one effect would be to alter democratic institutions in ways that may generate further democratic deficits and make it yet harder for individual citizens to feel engaged in government policy making. If the duty to consult applied to all legislative action, a private member of parliament or of a legislative assembly would be unlikely to be able to engage in consultation prior to introducing a private member's bill, with the effect that the use of private members' bills could become even more restricted, again raising fundamental questions about the effects on democracy. A private member is unlikely to be able to engage in the required consultation because a private member will not typically have sufficient resources to engage in extensive consultation on any legislation that affects multiple communities, and it would also become a problematic situation were there to be various private members seeking to consult Aboriginal communities in an uncoordinated way that might or might not match with other government consultation initiatives. That said, there might be some methods developed, but they would certainly pose extra challenges for private members seeking to introduce bills on often limited timelines within the lifespan of a parliament or legislature.

Moreover, the reform of any pieces of legislation having broad effects on Aboriginal communities, such as the *Indian Act* or such as any legislation related to Aboriginal education issues, could become even more hampered than at present if subject to the legal technicalities of the duty to consult. Quite simply, there are bound to be a variety of views in different Aboriginal communities, and the application of a technical legal doctrine concerning consultation at the very least complicates dramatically questions related to such legislative reform. Application of the duty to legislative action might seem like just a simple logical extension and a means of protecting Aboriginal communities, but there are possible arguments that it would have negative effects on democracy generally and on legislative reform in the very areas where Aboriginal communities need reform. In my view, the courts should remain extremely cautious in this particular context.

2.5 Consultation Partners

With whom is there a duty to consult? And by whom? These two questions sketch a set of surprisingly multifaceted problems.

2.5(a) Aboriginal Consultation Partner

First, in terms of to whom there is a duty to consult, the simple answer is that obligations are owed to rights-bearing communities whose rights may be affected by a particular government decision.

The duty to consult is owed by the Crown to Aboriginal communities. Communities are the main rights-holders under s. 35. Consequently, the duty to consult has almost universally been thought to be owed to communities rather than to individuals.[97] Indeed, where attempts have been made to litigate the duty to consult differently, such as through class representative proceedings rather than on behalf of a community, those alternative procedures have been rejected.[98] The issue of whether there is to be consultation with individuals, however, may not be fully closed. The Supreme Court of Canada's decision in *Behn* v. *Moulton Contracting*[99] saw arguments by the Grand Council of the Crees that some Aboriginal rights are individually held, with the possible implication that there might need to be consultation with individual Aboriginals.[100] To identify such rights would not be to say that there do not remain collective Aboriginal rights but to say that both collective and individual Aboriginal rights may well exist and that the courts need somehow to find ways of grappling with both.[101] But the Court's decision in *Behn* v. *Moulton Contracting* signalled a desire to avoid this question for the moment. So, for now, the historic pattern of communities being the sole rights-holders under s. 35 remains the necessary structuring thought for the duty to consult, with the result that consultation is to take place only with the representatives of rights-bearing communities.

In terms of the duty to consult rights-bearing communities, most of the duty to consult case law pertains to the duty to consult First Nations, and there is no doubt about the duty to consult First Nations whenever their Aboriginal or treaty rights trigger the duty to consult test. There is also clearly a duty to consult rights-bearing Inuit communities, as was held in a 2010 Nunavut case concerning scientific seismic testing that was alleged

---

97   *Lefthand, supra* note 3 at para 38.

98   *Campbell* v. *British Columbia, supra* note 74.

99   *Behn* v. *Moulton Contracting,* 2013 SCC 26.

100 *Ibid.*

101 *Ibid.*

to have the potential to have an impact on marine mammals in a manner that affected Inuit rights.[102]

Logically, there is also, of course, a duty to consult rights-bearing Métis communities concerning government decisions that affect constitutional Métis rights. That said, the concept of Métis rights remains relatively underdeveloped compared to that of Aboriginal rights held by First Nations, and there are even terminological confusions pervasive in the area. The Supreme Court of Canada signalled clearly in the *Powley* decision that there are such rights and even established the test for them.[103] However, the record of establishing such rights has been mixed, and has recently been subject to a major judicial setback in the *Hirsekorn* case in Alberta.[104] The case law development in this area, though, focuses on rights held by communities of Métis descended from historic Métis communities.[105] Sometimes different uses of the term "Métis," such as by individuals identifying themselves who are legally non-status Indians, complicate the discussion. The recent *Daniels* case from the Federal Court that concluded that Métis are "Indians" for purposes of s. 91(24) jurisdiction in the *Constitution Act, 1867* has not simplified matters in the public mind.[106] However, it is consistent with the position that the focus for these purposes is on historic Métis communities.

Claims that may be made on behalf of non-status Indians or other urban Aboriginal communities are less clear simply because the Aboriginal rights discourse in Canada has all developed around concepts of rights held by communities on account of historical practices, their occupation of traditional lands, and modern-day continuities from the past. However, were there to be the recognition of some form of Aboriginal right held by urban

---

102 *Qikiqtani Inuit Association v. Canada (Minister of Resources)*, 2010 NUCJ 12.

103 *R. v. Powley*, [2003] 2 S.C.R. 207, 2003 SCC 43.

104 *R. v. Hirsekorn*, 2013 ABCA 242, leave to appeal to Supreme Court of Canada refused 24 January 2014.

105 Thus, the rights will be regional in nature, which may affect duty to consult claims.

106 *Daniels v. Canada*, 2013 FC 6, varied on some points, 2014 FCA 101. For my discussion of the terminology, see Dwight Newman, "Of aboriginals, Métis, First Nations, Inuit, and Indians (status-holding and otherwise)," *National Post* (10 January 2013), available at http://fullcomment.nationalpost.com/2013/01/10/dwight-newman-of-aboriginals-metis-first-nations-inuit-and-indians-status-holding-and-otherwise.

Aboriginal communities, the duty to consult would then presumably apply to such a right, albeit with further complexities around the identification of the precise rights-bearing community and its appropriate representatives.[107]

A further complication in some contexts will be the identification of the appropriate Aboriginal consultation partner(s). It is clear that the courts intend that consultation be carried out with communities and not typically with potentially affected individuals, but the identification of the appropriate representatives of a community is not always a simple matter.[108] One issue arises in the context of representation by a province-wide organization. For example, in *Native Council of Nova Scotia* v. *Canada (Attorney General)*, the Federal Court ended up rejecting the Native Council of Nova Scotia as an inappropriate consultation partner because it included some non-Mi'kmaq members, although it otherwise represented Nova Scotia Mi'kmaq on a province-wide basis.[109] The Federal Court of Appeal in the same case held, however, that it was not necessary to decide on the matter, as there was a lack of evidence to support the asserted right in any event.[110]

In *Labrador Métis Nation* v. *Newfoundland and Labrador*,[111] the Newfoundland Court of Appeal considered a situation where a number of disparate communities in Labrador had not self-identified as either Inuit or Métis but had claims to rights flowing from Aboriginal ancestry that would apply to either category of Aboriginality. The Court held that the Crown ought to have recognized a credible claim that led to a triggering of the duty

---

107 See, generally, Dwight Newman, "The Duty to Consult Doctrine and Representative Structures for Métis Communities and Non-Status Indian Communities" (Ottawa: Institute on Governance, March 2010): http://lgdata.s3-website-us-east-1.amazonaws.com/docs/3978/794633/March2010_TheDutytoConsultDoctrine-Newman.pdf.

108 See *Red Chris Development Co.* v. *Quock*, 2006 BCSC 1472 at paras. 15-16, rejecting the claim of certain individuals who claimed they should have been consulted in addition to the elected leadership of the First Nation.

109 *Native Council of Nova Scotia* v. *Canada (Attorney General)*, 2007 FC 45, 306 F.T.R. 294 at paras. 43-44, aff'd, *supra* note 31.

110 *Supra* note 31 at paras. 3, 5.

111 *Labrador Métis Nation* v. *Newfoundland and Labrador (Minister of Transportation and Works)*, 2007 NLCA 75, 288 D.L.R. (4th) 641; leave to appeal to S.C.C. refused 32468 (29 May 2008).

to consult.[112] The Court was ready to accept the Labrador Métis Nation as an appropriate corporate agent to enforce the duty to consult through the lawsuit, seeing it as having been implicitly authorized by its members.[113] The Court also appears to have implicitly authorized that the form of consultation in the case could be appropriate notice to and opportunity to respond for the Labrador Métis Nation as a corporate body.[114] Thus, in some instances, Aboriginal communities without as much recognition in current governance structures will be able to constitute representative bodies that can fulfill their shared responsibilities in the consultation processes. This may represent an additional part of the solution to the capacity issues touched on above.

In its decision in *Re Imperial Oil Resources Ventures Ltd.*,[115] the Alberta Energy and Utilities Board applied conclusions from the Labrador Métis Nation litigation, while denying recognition to a number of groups asserting their claims to duties of consultation. The panel rejected the claims of two groups attempting to constitute themselves from individuals of already existing *Indian Act* bands, of an individual not connected to an Aboriginal community, and of an elders' society not showing itself to be the corporate agent of a rights-bearing Aboriginal community.[116] Corporate and government stakeholders tend to take the view that consultation with Métis communities would take place with Métis locals,[117] but there are complex and challenging questions on whether this is the preferable approach.[118] This topic will be subject to further discussion in Chapter 4, which examines briefly the policy frameworks enunciated by different Métis organizations.

---

112 *Ibid.* at para. 45.

113 *Ibid.* at paras. 46-47.

114 *Ibid.* at para. 52.

115 *Re Imperial Oil Resources Ventures Ltd.*, [2007] A.E.U.B.D. No. 13.

116 *Ibid.* at paras. 60-63.

117 The Métis Nation of Saskatchewan identified an instance in which a branch of the federal government was carrying on consultation with a committee appointed by the federal government as supposedly representative of Métis communities in the area: Thomas J. Bruner, "President of Métis Nation Demands Consultation," Saskatchewan Sage: The Aboriginal Newspaper of Saskatchewan (Mar. 2009), p. 3. Obviously, there is a legal error involved if the government seeks to consult with itself!

118 Jason Madden, unpublished conference paper.

The challenges are perhaps even more acute in the context of non-status Indians. The *Labrador Métis Nation* case opens the possibility of non-status communities being represented through appropriate representative organizations. The Congress of Aboriginal Peoples will presumably articulate a role for itself in this area, but the best representation of non-status communities on a particular issue may also be more localized. The duty to consult doctrine in some ways mandates a more formalized representative system as something that must be developed if Aboriginal communities are to benefit from consultation. If non-status communities do not formalize representative structures, they risk being further marginalized through the ongoing development of a doctrine that was intended to realize reconciliation with Aboriginal peoples.

This whole discussion on appropriate consultation partners raises additional issues. The government departments carrying out a consultation will need to assess carefully whether a particular body does or does not represent the relevant stakeholders. With the Native Council of Nova Scotia having been rejected but the Labrador Métis Nation having been recognized in cases that have entered into this area, the courts have not left things as clear as they could be. It is arguable, however, that the test implicit in the case law is whether the particular body either represents directly the interests of the relevant Aboriginal communities or is specifically authorized to do so, with an additional requirement in both cases being that it not be a representative body that represents potentially conflicting interests. This legal position creates some genuine practical challenges in implementation that will need to be worked through in the years ahead.

Finally, it is worth noting that the complexity of Aboriginal communities and their claims means that there will often be overlapping Aboriginal claims that will sometimes be in tension. In such situations, there may be a duty to consult with different Aboriginal communities, including about how rights fulfillment for one community affects another. For example, in *Sambaa K'e Dene Band* v. *Duncan*,[119] agreement on a land claim with one First Nation properly gave rise to consultation in relation to other First Nations with overlapping claims. Such types of overlaps could conceivably in some cases appear to lessen the *prima facie* strength of a claim, affecting the depth of a consultation duty, but they will not typically eliminate

---

119 *Sambaa K'e Dene Band* v. *Duncan*, 2012 FC 204.

the duty to consult.[120] In *Enge* v. *Mandeville*,[121] the Northwest Territories Supreme Court considered competing claims of Métis and First Nations in relation to caribou hunting and held that although the approval of a First Nations harvesting plan was not automatically wrong, there was a duty to consult the Métis community that appeared also to have a *prima facie* Aboriginal Métis hunting right. Thus, there is a duty to consult any Aboriginal community with an Aboriginal or treaty right, and the communities that hold such rights may be more complex than first realized and may even hold overlapping or competing rights.

Once initiated, a duty to consult creates a set of shared responsibilities between the Crown and Aboriginal communities. If an Aboriginal community does not engage fully in a consultation process, for example, it may limit the Crown's duty to consult. In *Ahousaht Indian Band* v. *Canada (Minister of Fisheries & Oceans)*,[122] the First Nation's representative on an advisory committee did not attend early meetings of the committee. With the First Nation entering into the process late, and later delaying matters by insisting on the adoption of a consultation protocol, the Crown did not breach the duty to consult when it went ahead with a plan for commercial fishing without further bilateral discussions.[123] If an Aboriginal community indicates that it has acquiesced to a particular consultation procedure, this will also be a factor that may limit further consultation requirements on the part of the Crown.[124] Finally, if repeated requests for input from an Aboriginal community go unanswered, case law suggests this may terminate further requirements in the duty to consult on the issue on which those requests have been made.[125]

The responsibilities of the Aboriginal consultation partner will in some instances create real challenges for the community. In a small office, Aboriginal leaders may be expected to be simultaneously developing negotiation strategies on issues with the Crown, considering litigation in some issues, and now dealing with consultation issues. In some instances, consultation will involve significant quantities of paperwork, increas-

---

120 *Louis, supra* note 53, at paras. 73, 89.

121 *Enge* v. *Mandeville*, [2013] 4 C.N.L.R. 50 (N.W.T.S.C.).

122 *Ahousaht Indian Band, supra* note 32.

123 *Ibid.*

124 *Paul First Nation* v. *Parkland (County)*, 2006 ABCA 128, [2006] C.N.L.R. 243.

125 *Lefthand, supra* note 3 at para. 43. Cf. also *Douglas, supra* note 38 at para 45.

ing as individuals seeking to avoid the risk of being accused of insufficient consultation add additional paperwork to what is sent out. Some of the panel members in the British Columbia Environmental Appeal Board May 2008 decision involving the Xats'ull First Nation's challenge to a mining discharge permit noted this challenge. Panel member Derkaz wrote in her dissenting opinion:

> [I]t is clear from the evidence of Mr. Michel and Mr. Phillips that the Xats'ull lack the financial and technical capacity to deal with the numerous referrals from companies seeking to carry on industrial activities that may affect their aboriginal interests. I have sympathy for the Xats'ull staff who are trying to deal with complicated applications without adequate resources. It is an unequal, and perhaps inherently unfair, relationship. This lack of capacity must be addressed if the province is going to live up to the vision expressed in the New Relationship with aboriginal people. However this is a matter beyond the jurisdiction of this Board.[126]

There will be times where it is appropriate that funding be made available to assist with consultation where the challenges are partly financial. Indeed, the Supreme Court of Canada's creation of the duty to consult has risked imposing on many Aboriginal communities quite costly activities that could have drawn on the same resource pool in use for longer-term negotiations and/or litigation. Many consultations will be technically complex, generating additional costs. The Métis Nation of Saskatchewan, to take one example, has estimated at $40,000 the costs it incurred in consulting with the Canadian Nuclear Safety Commission about abandoned uranium mines.[127] Some First Nations receive hundreds or even thousands of consultation requests each year. In light of these challenges, several provinces have moved to make funding available to facilitate consultation processes. However, merely making funding available is not necessarily a solution to some complex challenges. It is, in any case, clear that the capacity to engage in consultation flowing from the duty to consult is a real issue in the context of some Aboriginal communities' situations.

---

126 *Xats'ull First Nation* v. *Director, Environmental Management Act*, 2006-EMA-006(a), at para. 412: www.eab.gov.bc.ca/ema/2006ema006a.pdf.

127 Luke Simcoe, "Duty to consult should include funding: MNS," *Saskatoon StarPhoenix* (16 Mar. 2009), A3.

2.5(b) Government Consultation Partner

Turning to the second question at stake in this section, in terms of by whom the duty is owed, it is clear in basic terms that the constitutional duty to consult is a duty owed by the Crown. One of the Supreme Court of Canada's decisions in the *Haida Nation* case was that the Court of Appeal's judgement that would have imposed the duty to consult on third parties was without legal foundation. Chief Justice McLachlin made clear that the Crown alone bears ultimate responsibility under the duty to consult:

> The Crown alone remains legally responsible for the consequences of its actions and interactions with third parties, that affect Aboriginal interests. The Crown may delegate procedural aspects of consultation to industry proponents seeking a particular development; this is not infrequently done in environmental assessments. Similarly, the terms of T.F.L. 39 mandated Weyerhaeuser to specify measures that it would take to identify and consult with "aboriginal people claiming an aboriginal interest in or to the area" (Tree Farm Licence No. 39, Haida Tree Farm Licence, para. 2.09(g)(ii)). However, the ultimate legal responsibility for consultation and accommodation rests with the Crown. The honour of the Crown cannot be delegated.[128]

The possibility of delegation that is contained within this passage does mean that third parties can become involved. But the fundamental point is that the duty is owed by the Crown.

The constitutional duty to consult is one owed in a certain sense by an undivided Crown. The Crown can fail to meet its constitutional duties through problematic division of information within government as surely as through more deliberate failures to consult. If some departments are not well acquainted with consultation requirements, then they must seek advice from others. There must also be a sharing of information within government in respect of likely Aboriginal title, Aboriginal rights, and treaty rights claims.

The Crown, for these purposes, can be either the federal Crown or the provincial Crown. Whichever government has jurisdiction over a particular decision that may affect Aboriginal or treaty rights will be the govern-

---

128 *Haida Nation, supra* note 1 at para. 53.

ment that owes the duty to consult. In practical terms, many decisions on resource issues will be made by provincial governments due to the primary provincial jurisdiction over matters of natural resources — albeit with significant exceptions in such areas as interprovincial transportation of resources and areas like uranium development where the federal government has additional bases for jurisdiction.[129] So, provincial governments will very often be involved in decisions on which there needs to be consultation with Aboriginal communities.

In some cases, there may be a need for the involvement of both the federal and provincial governments. A peculiar situation of this type arose in the *Ehattesaht First Nation* case.[130] In this case, a recent division of powers determination had been made that aquaculture belonged in federal jurisdiction rather than in provincial jurisdiction as had previously been assumed, with the result that both the provincial and federal governments were taking steps in the same area. As a result, the conduct of both the federal Crown and the provincial Crown was at issue. In the peculiar circumstances of the case, the various duty to consult issues could not even all be heard by the same court, because some belonged within the provincial superior court system and some within the federal court system. Depending on the circumstances and the rules governing the jurisdiction of the Federal Court, either the provincial superior court system (the Court of Queen's Bench, in most provinces, though the Supreme Court in British Columbia) or the Federal Court system may have jurisdiction in a particular duty to consult case, to be determined on the basis of jurisdictional rules beyond the scope of this book.[131]

In Canadian constitutional terms, municipal governments do not have separate constitutional status but are creations of the provincial governments. An interesting, and possibly even surprising, decision was rendered by the British Columbia Court of Appeal concerning municipal

---

129 For discussion of jurisdiction on natural resource questions, see generally Dwight Newman, *Natural Resource Jurisdiction in Canada* (Toronto: Lexis-Nexis, 2013).

130 *Ehattesaht Frst Nation* v. *British Columbia (Minister of Agriculture and Lands)*, 2011 BCSC 658, leave to appeal to British Columbia Court of Appeal refused 28 June 2011.

131 See *Tzeachten First Nation* v. *Canada (Attorney General)*, 2007 BCCA 133, 281 D.L.R. (4th) 752, rev'g. *Tzeachten First Nation* v. *Canada (Attorney General)*, 2006 BCSC 479, [2006] 6 W.W.R. 113.

governments and the duty to consult in the case of *Neskonlith Indian Band* v. *City of Salmon Arm* in late 2012.[132] The broad reading of the case is that the British Columbia Court of Appeal held that municipal governments do not have a duty to consult. However, that overly broad reading does not explain the case especially well. As explained in Chapter 1, a key determination of the Supreme Court of Canada in the *Rio Tinto* case[133] was that administrative bodies created by federal or provincial governments have a role in relation to the duty to consult as and only as defined by their originating statutes. The same principle applies, in the end, in respect of municipal governments. The British Columbia Court of Appeal was not ready to read in a role of the municipal government to engage in consultation where its originating statute did not leave enough room to establish such a role. There had previously been an analogous decision of the Alberta Court of Appeal. In a case concerning the actions of a municipal board carrying out land development, the Alberta Court of Appeal suggested that a municipal entity is not expected to carry out a more extended consultation than that within the processes set out for it within its statutes.[134]

That said, the statutes concerning urban and rural municipalities may, of course, differ in other provinces such that municipalities do indeed have a responsibility to engage in consultation, or they could be amended in that way. Having that role for municipalities on decisions that they make might well be efficient. An absence of consultation by the municipality would leave the provincial Crown subject to a claim that a duty of consultation had not been fulfilled unless the provincial government were set up so as to be approving municipal decisions following any legally required consultation. Thus, the relationship of municipal governments to consultation will be based on their originating statutes; no outcome avoids the duty to consult but each possible approach simply locates the duty to consult differently.

---

132 *Neskonlith Indian Band* v. *City of Salmon Arm,* [2012] 4 C.N.L.R. 218.

133 *Rio Tinto, supra* note 7.

134 *Paul First Nation, supra* note 124 at paras. 7, 12.

2.5(c) Role of Administrative Tribunals and of Courts

The basic rule on the role of administrative tribunals is now stated in *Rio Tinto*: "The duty on a tribunal to consider consultation and the scope of that inquiry depends on the mandate conferred by the legislation that creates the tribunal."[135] Some tribunals can actually be set up to be responsible to carry out consultation. Some can be set up to assess consultation carried out by others. And some have no role on consultation. In the last case, the duty to consult does not disappear. The government is always obligated to organize itself so that the legally required consultation occurs somehow. The courts simply will not dictate that form of organization, and the government's statutory mandates for each administrative board or tribunal determine what that particular part of government does. Where a particular administrative body is expressly exempted from being involved in consultation, then it will not be expected to be involved in consultation.[136]

Apart from the main government consultation policies, where administrative bodies such as the National Energy Board have adopted consultation policies, they have also been ready to enforce the constitutional duty to consult. If there are reasonable consultation efforts under way, the National Energy Board has in some instances been quite non-interventionist, content to suggest that it "strongly supports the development of such arrangements [ongoing consultation activities and efforts to develop agreements] and encourages project proponents to build relationships with Aboriginal groups with interests in the area of their projects."[137]

Where appropriate, the National Energy Board has also been ready to scrutinize matters more closely. As just one example, in February 2008, the Board released its decision in *Re Enbridge Pipelines Inc.*,[138] in which it considered an application by Enbridge concerning the construction and operation of the Alberta Clipper pipeline project. In its hearings, the National Energy Board heard from a number of Aboriginal parties, including the Standing Buffalo Dakota Nation, the Roseau River Anishinabe

---

135 *Rio Tinto, supra* note 7 at para. 55.

136 *Métis Nation of Alberta Region 1* v. *Shell Canada Energy*, 2012 ABCA 352, leave to appeal refused 11 April 2013.

137 *Re TransCanada Keystone Pipeline GP Ltd.* (Sept. 2007), 2007 LNCNEB 9, OH-1-2007 at para. 155 (N.E.B.).

138 *Re Enbridge Pipelines Inc.* (Feb. 2008), 2008 LNCNEB 2, OH-4-2007 (N.E.B.).

Nation, the Samson Cree Nation, the Maskwacis Cree Nation, the Manitoba Métis Federation, and the Montana First Nation,[139] and eventually a number of others.[140] The Board showed some reluctance to evaluate the legal adequacy of Crown consultations,[141] but was ready to consider Aboriginal interests prior to reaching a decision.[142] It was also ready to consider whether the proponent had engaged in consultation fitting with the policies enunciated by the National Energy Board, and to include conditions on approval that there be ongoing updates on consultation with Aboriginal communities, and that special rules would enter into play in the event of the finding of undiscovered historical, archeological, and burial sites.[143]

Similarly, in a March 2009 decision concerning an application by SemCAMS Redwillow ULC to construct and operate a sour gas pipeline from northeastern British Columbia to facilities near Grand Prairie, Alberta,[144] the National Energy Board was ready to elaborate a substantial set of conditions and become involved in the ongoing monitoring of them. The Board was ready to direct ongoing consultation with potentially affected Aboriginal communities throughout the project's lifetime, filing monthly reports during the construction phase on consultation, concerns raised, and how these were addressed.[145] Thus, in some instances, there is the potential for administrative boards and tribunals with particular expertise to enter into closer monitoring of duty to consult issues. The National Energy Board has continued to seek to foster good consultation practices. For example, in its recent report on the Northern Gateway Pipeline, it speaks to the importance of ongoing consultation, embodying many good principles on consultation.[146] That

---

139 *Ibid.* at para. 15, which lists Aboriginal parties that provided input during the hearing.

140 *Ibid.* at para. 118, which sets out a number of intervenors at a later hearing.

141 *Ibid.* at para. 30.

142 *Ibid.* at para. 50.

143 *Ibid.* at para. 150.

144 *Re SemCAMS Redwillow* ULC (Mar. 2009), 2009 LNCNEB 3, No. GH-2-2008 (N.E.B.).

145 *Ibid.* at para. 125.

146 See *Report of the Joint Review Panel for the Enbridge Northern Gateway Project* (Calgary: National Energy Board, 2013), vol. 2: Considerations, ch. 4: Aborig-

last report, notably, does not end the consultation process but speaks to it continuing so as to meet its objectives, some of which have been further fleshed out again in the special Eyford Report.[147]

The constitutional duty to consult is an obligation intended to foster negotiation and nation-to-nation relationships over judicial dispute resolution processes. However, where everything has gone wrong, the constitutional nature of the duty does mean that it can be enforced through administrative tribunals that have the power to adjudicate upon it or through the courts if there are concerns about the way in which consultations have (or have not) been pursued in particular circumstances.

First, it is essential to realize that the courts are not the sole option. Quasi-judicial administrative boards and tribunals will, where it falls within their jurisdiction, review other government actors' efforts at consultation.[148] Indeed, there has been a specific rejection of some boards' previous "aversion to assessing the adequacy of consultation"[149] and an indication that such quasi-judicial bodies have "the obligation ... to decide the constitutional question of whether the duty to consult exists and, if so, whether it has been discharged."[150] Many administrative boards and tribunals have in fact been making rulings on the acceptability or unacceptability of certain consultation processes.[151] It is also sometimes possible for such bodies to enter into supervision of fairly detailed terms they may impose on governments or other parties in relation to consultation as part of their regulatory approval processes.[152]

---

inal interests and consultation with Aboriginal groups: http://gatewaypanel. review-examen.gc.ca/clf-nsi/dcmnt/rcmndtnsrprt/rcmndtnsrprt-eng.html.

147 Douglas R. Eyford, Report to the Prime Minister: *Forging Partnerships, Building Relationships: Aboriginal Canadians and Energy Development* (29 November 2013): https://www.nrcan.gc.ca/sites/www.nrcan.gc.ca/files/www/pdf/publications/ForgPart-Online-e.pdf.

148 See, generally, *Kwikwetlem First Nation* v. *British Columbia (Utilities Commission)*, 2009 BCCA 68 at paras. 8, 13-15.

149 *Carrier Sekani Tribal Council* v. *British Columbia (Utilities Commission)*, 2009 BCCA 67 at para. 14, affirmed by *Rio Tinto, supra* note 7.

150 *Ibid.* at para. 15. See also *Kwikwetlem First Nation, supra* note 148 at paras. 13-15.

151 An example is *Re SemCAMS Redwillow ULC, supra* note 144 at para. 125.

152 See, for example, *Penelakut First Nation Elders* v. *British Columbia (Ministry of Water, Land and Air Protection)*, [2004] B.C.E.A. No. 34 (B.C.E.A.B.) at paras.

Once intervention in a duty to consult is under consideration, it is important to understand something of the possible remedies. First, before turning to remedies in relation to the duty to consult itself, in urgent circumstances a motion could be brought to restrain activities that would have an adverse effect on an Aboriginal community even prior to a judicial decision on the duty to consult.[153] Once one of the parties has concluded that there is a problem with the consultation process, the remedy depends in many respects on what stage matters have reached. In one sense, the appropriate remedy to insufficient consultation in a circumstance where consultation can still be ordered is to order that consultation.[154] This may be the case even where matters are some way along; in some circumstances it has been held appropriate to appoint a mediator if consultation is proving ineffective.[155] The courts will also sometimes engage in ongoing court supervision of consultation.[156]

Where decisions have already been made, the question may arise as to whether they should be stopped. As in other areas of law, the courts will typically not restrain dispositions of specific land where there is nothing unique about that land.[157] There will be other contexts in which the remedy for a breach of the duty to consult that is a *fait accompli* is damages,[158] possibly at an elevated level that contains a punitive element against a government if its conduct has been blameworthy.[159]

A court faced with the question of how to remedy a failure to meet the standards of the duty to consult obviously seeks to try to remedy the wrong, but should do so in a manner that is practical and fair to all who

---

147-48, 151-83.

153 *Kruger Inc.* v. *Betsiamites First Nation*, 2006 QCCA 569, [2006] 3 C.N.L.R. 19 (an injunction granted by a lower court resulting in delay in development until after a Court of Appeal decision; leave to appeal *Kruger Inc.* to S.C.C. refused 384 N.R. 195 (20 Oct. 2005)) at paras. 47, 50.

154 *Lefthand, supra* note 3 at para. 165, per Conrad J. A.

155 *Ke-Kin-is-Uqs, supra* note 80 at paras. 255-256.

156 *Lameman* v. *Alberta*, 2013 ABCA 148.

157 *Musqueam Indian Band* v. *Canada*, 2008 FCA 214, 297 D.L.R. (4th) 349 at paras. 45-46, 58-58, 297, leave to appeal to Supreme Court of Canada refused 32785 (4 Dec. 2008).

158 See *Ke-Kin-is-Uqs, supra* note 80 at paras. 231-32. Cf. *Musqueam Indian Band, ibid.* at paras. 48, 58.

159 Cf. *Haida Nation, supra* note 1 at para. 76.

are affected by the remedy, including third-party stakeholders who played no role in the Crown's failure to meet its duties.[160] In some instances, the complex considerations at play may warrant a separate remedies hearing, at which it would presumably be possible to carefully consider the impact of different possible remedies on all stakeholders.[161] Some courts have indicated a reluctance to quash government decisions in instances where doing so may not be in the best interests of developments that may benefit everyone, including the Aboriginal communities involved.[162]

One new area of case law that has arisen very recently is the possibility that non-Aboriginal parties will sue over duty to consult issues. Specifically, in some situations in which governments have failed to carry out their duty to consult obligations, industry stakeholders have indicated intentions to sue to recover losses sustained as a result.[163] What will come of these suits remains to be seen as they progress through the courts or are settled.

What all of these issues about remedies share in common, however, is that if these questions are reached, that very fact marks a failure in the process and, to some extent, in the doctrine itself. Happily, the case law that has developed in the courts on the duty to consult, substantial as it is, represents a fraction of the situations in which consultations have occurred, with results reasonably satisfactory (or better) on all sides. The duty to consult doctrine has developed precisely as a means to avoid extra litigation and as a means of fostering better relationships and negotiated agreements. While it is necessary to have some ideas as to possible remedies that lower courts have identified, it is preferable if this particular aspect of the case law is relevant as seldom as possible.

2.6 Role of Project Proponents

Although the Crown bears ultimate responsibility for the duty to consult, the duty to consult may have significant implications for third parties, which may, in turn, be of concern to governments from an economic de-

---

160 *Dene Tha' (Fed. Ct.)*, *supra* note 56 at para. 119. See also *Ke-Kin-is-Uqs, supra* note 80 at paras. 261-63.

161 *Dene Tha' (Fed. Ct.)*, *ibid.* at paras. 133-34.

162 *Ka'a'gee Tu First Nation v. Canada (Minister of Indian & Northern Affairs)*, 2007 FC 764, [2008] 2 F.C.R. 473 at paras. 73-75.

163 Examples of such lawsuits will be discussed later in the book.

velopment perspective. The decisions to which the duty to consult applies often have very significant implications for a range of stakeholders. Considering simply a more extreme example, in *Dene Tha' First Nation* v. *Canada (Minister of Environment)*, a failure to consult First Nations about the Mackenzie Gas Project led to an interim injunction against further steps on the project.[164] In reality, the delays occasioned by consultation may well have killed the project, at least for now, even where it was one that would have generated economic benefits for the region generally and it had drawn the support of a number of Aboriginal groups who had taken an equity-type role in the project. The stakes are high for project proponents, for Aboriginal communities, and for Canadians generally in duty to consult situations affecting major projects.

In situations where there has not been adequate consultation, protests and even blockades have emerged, with Indigenous communities claiming that particular developments have not complied with consultation requirements.[165] Whether the duty to consult is met may have major implications for whether there is a social licence to operate in respect of a particular project. In Chapter 4 it is argued that, although the duty to consult does not apply to third parties in Canadian case law, an emerging practice of industry stakeholders and Aboriginal communities is nonetheless making corporate consultation with Aboriginal communities a non-optional practice.

The Crown in any event has the option of involving third parties — most likely the corporations involved in a project under consideration — in actually carrying out a consultation. Different industry stakeholders hold different views about this. Some were pleased by the decisions of some governments, like that of Saskatchewan, that consultation would be carried out solely by governments. Others indicated that they would like

---

164 *Dene Tha' (Fed. Ct.), supra* note 56 at paras. 133-34. See also *Homalco Indian Band* v. *British Columbia (Minister of Agriculture, Food & Fisheries)*, 2005 BCSC 283, 39 B.C.L.R. (4th) 263 at para. 108, temporarily restraining placement of further fish in a farming operation, until government fulfilled the duty to consult; and *Kruger Inc.* v. *Betsiamites First Nation, supra* note 153, an injunction granted by a lower court resulting in delay in development until after a Court of Appeal decision; leave to appeal Kruger Inc. to S.C.C. refused 384 N.R. 195 (20 Oct. 2005).

165 See, for example, *Frontenac Ventures Corp.* v. *Ardoch Algonquin First Nation*, [2008] CarswellOnt 1168 (Ont. Sup Ct.), a company seeking an injunction when not able to carry out mining.

to have more of a role in consultations. What will work best on this front may depend on circumstances and relationships in different provinces, as well as the nature of the matters on which Aboriginal communities are to be consulted.

Much of how this proceeds will actually remain to be defined by the policies and practices of governments and Aboriginal communities. One danger of having different industry stakeholders involved in carrying out consultations is that it may become difficult for an Aboriginal community to identify when it is or is not engaged in discussions that amount to consultation for purposes of the duty to consult. Various industry representatives may engage in discussions that might later be portrayed as part of a consultation process. This worry can be overcome by the government either carrying out all consultation itself or delegating its consultation roles quite explicitly where it does so. There will sometimes be advantages in delegating consultation. An industry stakeholder that is a proponent for a project will have a strong interest in seeing that consultation takes place efficiently and in accordance with the law. It may also have a very clear sense on the costs of different options for accommodation in a particular circumstance, and whether they will affect the viability of the project. The particular modalities of consultation delegated to third parties will be worked out not through further case law so much as through the policies and practices discussed in Chapter 4.

2.7 Negotiated Alternatives to the Duty to Consult

The duty to consult is a background constitutional duty that applies to government decisions that affect Aboriginal or treaty rights. However, sometimes the legal formalities of the duty to consult will not be what best serves anyone involved in a particular decision, including the Aboriginal communities affected. The duty to consult case law has developed in particular ways that may or may not best meet the needs of certain regions. As a result, one major negotiated alternative to the duty to consult arises in the context of modern treaties, many of which contain provisions specifying certain consultation regimes that may differ from the basic duty to consult framework.

As explained earlier in the chapter, modern treaties' more specific terms may well end up shaping the duty to consult in their particular regions. As stated in *Beckman* v. *Little Salmon/Carmacks First Nation*:

When a modern treaty has been concluded, the first step is to look at its provisions and try to determine the parties' respective obligations, and whether there is some form of consultation provided for in the treaty itself. If a process of consultation has been established in the treaty, the scope of the duty to consult will be shaped by its provisions.[166]

Treaty terms in modern, detailed agreements can shape the consultation mechanisms appropriate to a particular region. In many instances, these terms go beyond what would arise under the background constitutional duty to consult or at least take matters in more specific directions that the courts could not compel. For example, in many of the modern treaties, there is not simple consultation on wildlife management in a traditional territory but rather the establishment of joint governance mechanisms related to wildlife management. The ultimate solutions to challenges faced by Indigenous communities are not actually likely to come from the courts, nor should they. They will come from broader processes of societal reconciliation. The background pressure of the duty to consult doctrine, however, may encourage the continuing development of positive arrangements where we can find paths forward together.

Importantly, the negotiated arrangements with Aboriginal communities will not all be arrangements with governments. They may, rather, be deals struck with private enterprise. The duty to consult, as will be discussed in Chapter 3, can be an important lever to such deals. A range of different levels of deals can be struck, ultimately culminating in an impact benefit agreement between an industry stakeholder and an Aboriginal community. Such an impact benefit agreement may actually resolve consultation issues in respect of a particular project and, indeed, may contain terms precisely designed to do so.

In part simply to face up to various legal uncertainties and in part to address any risks arising from the duty to consult, many responsible resource companies now engage with Aboriginal communities and pursue good relationships with the hope also of negotiating win-win arrangements for economic development. An appropriately developed impact benefit agreement (IBA) may provide gains for all. While it yields protections and economic benefits for an Aboriginal community, it may offer greater certainty for an industry stakeholder and may also offer other benefits, such as ar-

---

166 *Beckman* v. *Little Salmon/Carmacks First Nation*, 2010 SCC 53, [2010] 3 S.C.R. 103, at para. 67.

rangements to bolster a trained labour force in a remote region in which resource development is to occur.

Not all IBAs, of course, are public. But some are. On the legal certainty point, IBAs may contain a "support clause." One recent agreement between a mining company and a northern mixed First Nations and Métis community provides an example, with the support clause alone stretching over three pages, but with some subclauses, including the following:

> [the community] acknowledges in general that it has been consulted over the course of many years in relation to the Existing Operations, that it is well informed as to the general nature of the Existing Operations, that its Residents have been given many opportunities over the years to learn about and to express concerns about the Existing Operations, and that it fully supports the Existing Operations and the Existing Authorizations [...]
> in respect of Proposed Projects and Proposed Authorizations [...]
> [the community] fully supports [the companies] in continuing with their respective plans for the Proposed Projects and seeking to obtain the Proposed Authorizations;
> (ii) [the community] acknowledges in general that, to date, it has been consulted broadly by [the company] and applicable governmental authorities regarding the proposed [...] project, that it is well informed as to the general nature of the proposed [...] project, that its Residents have been given opportunities to learn about and to express concerns about the proposed [...] project, and that, subject to sub-section 5.1(b)(iii) it intends to fully support the [...] project;
> (iii) provided that [the companies] implement their obligations around consulting and engaging [the community] as set out in Schedule F regarding any such Proposed Projects and Proposed Authorizations (which, for the avoidance of doubt, involves meaningfully addressing relevant [community] concerns raised in accordance with the processes set out in Schedule F or otherwise), [the community] intends to fully support the Proposed Projects and acknowledges it will be a breach of this Agreement to oppose the issuance of any Proposed Authorizations or the construction, development or operation of any of the Proposed Projects; and
> (iv) for the avoidance of doubt, nothing in this sub-section or in any

other term of this Agreement, precludes [the community] or its Residents from raising concerns in any forum or to any entity whatsoever regarding Proposed Projects or Proposed Authorizations [...].[167]

Similar parts of the agreement also provide support for exploration activities, subject to compliance with various commitments to the community. Sources have indicated that this particular support clause (or one similar to it) has been used in other agreements also, including by a prominent practitioner in the field, although most such agreements end up not being publicly disclosed. The clause's effect that opposition by the community to a project would become a breach of the agreement, thus conceivably subjecting the community to remedies that might include denial of the benefits provided under the agreement, may appear controversial to some. However, the hope obviously is to develop legal commitments that are consistent with an ongoing relationship that works well for all involved. The effect, however, is to allow a negotiation of a substitute for the duty to consult. That is not necessarily a bad thing, however, and may simply say that the arrangements in question may actually offer something better than the legal technicalities of the duty to consult doctrine which has helped foster such agreements.

2.8 Conclusion

The lower courts developing the duty to consult case law pursuant to McLachlin C.J.'s guidance have been confronted with a number of pragmatic questions and have had to make a potentially theoretical and abstract doctrine work in the circumstances of real life. They have adopted some additional restraints on the triggering of the duty to avoid an impractical imposition of the duty to consult in an enormous range of circumstances. They have addressed some complex questions on the appropriate partners within a consultation, and they have generally sought to develop their jurisprudence in a manner that makes the duty to consult work effectively in the context of real-life considerations. Making the duty to consult workable does not mean retreating from its aspirations; rather, it means

---

167 This clause comes from a publicly available document. However, to respect the privacy of the companies and the community, I have excerpted their names and will not cite to the specific document here. That said, the document is readily available to those who seek it.

fulfilling them and making them accessible. In the process, however, the highly generalized language of the Supreme Court of Canada has had to be attuned to real circumstances.

3

The Doctrinal Scope and Content
of the Duty to Consult

3.1 Introduction

The previous chapter set out the legal parameters of the duty to consult, including the contexts in which a duty to consult arises and who is engaged in the processes flowing from that duty. To understand the duty, however, the next question is that of the scope and content of the duty to consult. What does it require?

The content of the duty in particular circumstances varies based on certain factors, with the courts thus having conceptualized it in terms of a spectrum analysis. As with any legal test that relies on multiple factors, there is a great deal of space for interpretation of the specific requirements in particular instances. This chapter, then, attempts to give the implications of this spectrum analysis more specific shape. It then goes on to say something about the particular circumstances in which the duty to consult gives rise to duties of accommodation and the even more particular circumstances in which accommodation takes an economic form. Finally, the chapter turns to why all involved may actually wish to reach above the law and may better live out the purposes of the duty to consult and achieve better win-win solutions by rising above legal technicalities.

At a fundamental, principled level, the aim in any consultation context is to achieve *meaningful* consultation. Meaningful consultation is that which achieves the purposes of the doctrine. The duty to consult doctrine seeks to maintain honourable Crown conduct and to offer a proactive protection to Aboriginal and treaty rights such that in situations of uncertainty about the scope of Aboriginal and treaty rights, there is discussion of that uncertainty in advance of a government decision that may adversely impact them. These underlying objects receive protection through a mechanism of providing appropriate notice and information concerning the contemplated government decision, offering an opportunity for response to and feedback on that decision, and government engaging in appropriate consideration of that response.[1]

Although one could draw some more complex distinctions if one carried out the comparison at length, there are analogies here to basic ideas of common law administrative law. Administrative law governs more generally the way in which governments make decisions when these decisions affect individuals. A duty of procedural fairness arises in situations where governments in these public relations with individuals have a duty of care to those individuals. Some of the most basic elements of procedural fairness in such situations include a right to contextually appropriate notice,[2] a right to disclosure of appropriate information in the context of that notice,[3] and a right to be heard (*audi alterem partem*) in the sense of having an opportunity to respond to that notice in a contextually appropriate way and to have that response considered.[4]

Meaningful consultation will take different forms in different circumstances, being the form of consultation that is necessary to enable an appropriate level of respect for Aboriginal and treaty rights via enabling a genuine process for the type of feedback that is most appropriate in given circumstances and that fosters the government taking proper account of that feedback.[5] This standard of meaningful consultation does not mean that there will necessarily be ultimate agreement on every issue. Failure to agree on a particular issue does not necessarily imply that consultation has

---

1   Cf. *Haida Nation* v. *British Columbia (Minister of Forests)*, [2004] 3 S.C.R. 511, 2004 SCC 73 at para. 41.

2   Cf. *Canada (Attorney General)* v. *Canada (Commission of Inquiry on the Blood System in Canada)*, [1997] 3 SCR 440 at paras. 70-71; *Canadian Pacific Railway Company* v. *Vancouver (City)*, 2006 SCC 5, [2006] 1 SCR 227.

3   Cf. *May* v. *Ferndale Institution*, 2005 SCC 82, [2005] 3 SCR 809, at paras. 89-100.

4   Cf. *Nicholson* v. *Haldimand Norfolk (Regional) Police Commissioners*, [1979] 1 SCR 311.

5   On the significance of consultation enabling that opportunity for feedback, see generally *White River First Nation* v. *Yukon (Minister of Energy, Mines, and Resources)*, 2013 YKSC 66.

been unsuccessful so long as everyone involved has attempted it genuinely in good faith and with the aspiration of meaningful consultation that tries to reach agreement on means of respecting the Aboriginal and treaty rights at issue.[6] There is also not meant to be any unrealistic process, but rather a contextually appropriate one, and in some circumstances, meaningful consultation will have been achieved simply by offering affected Aboriginal communities an opportunity to review a government decision document.[7] What is essential is compliance with the general requirements of meaningful consultation, carried out in good faith, and that the government not short-circuit the process, for example, arbitrarily declaring it finished in some way that does not respect the demands of the process.[8]

Meaningful consultation, it bears noting, is a legal concept and a legal requirement on consultation processes under the duty to consult. A *good* consultation need not and arguably ought not to be limited to the elements prescribed by legal doctrine. Good consultations are about developing relationships and finding ways of living together in the encounter that history has thrust upon us. Pursuing legally acceptable *meaningful* consultation is an important step in that process and has much to offer compared to the situation prior to having the duty to consult doctrine. At the same time, focusing too narrowly on the legal form of the duty may contain hidden dangers to deeper forms of reconciliation. Focusing on the legal doctrine may result in a legalistic approach to relationships that entails extensive attempts to formalize and document discussions, which might well not be what best contributes to a relationship of trust. Later in this chapter, we will return to attempting to characterize a good consultation, with part of the suggestion being the importance of going beyond the elements prescribed by legal doctrine.

---

6   See generally *Ka'a'Gee Tu First Nation* v. *Canada (Attorney General)*, 2012 FC 297, 406 F.T.R. 229.

7   See e.g. *Liard First Nation* v. *Yukon (Minister of Energy, Mines and Resources)*, 2011 YKSC 55.

8   See e.g. *Cold Lake First Nation* v. *Alberta (Minister of Tourism, Parks and Recreation)*, 2012 ABQB 579, [2013] 1 C.N.L.R. 12, reversed on other aspects by 2013 ABCA 443, which arguably heightens this standard somewhat but without changing what has already been stated. Application for leave to appeal to the Supreme Court of Canada was filed on 18 February 2014 and not yet decided as of this writing.

3.2 Content of the Duty to Consult — The Spectrum Analysis

The triggering of a duty to consult in particular circumstances opens the further question of the content of the legal duty in those circumstances, as it can range from a fairly minimal consultation to a thorough duty to consult Aboriginal communities in a deep manner and to fully accommodate their interests. The reason for this range of possible content is to seek to respond appropriately to the purposes of the duty to consult in different contexts where less or more consultation is necessary in order to fulfill these purposes. The Supreme Court of Canada, in an attempt to make the doctrine easier to use and understand, offers a spectrum analysis. But this spectrum analysis should not be thought to replace the underlying purposes of the doctrine and is simply a tool for attempting to fulfill those purposes. As put by McLachlin C.J.C. in *Haida Nation*, "the concept of a spectrum may be helpful, not to suggest watertight legal compartments but rather to indicate what the honour of the Crown may require in particular circumstances."[9]

Throughout the spectrum, situations require a meaningful effort by the government to act in a manner consistent with the honour of the Crown.[10] This means that the government must act adequately for the circumstances in providing notice of an issue and appropriate timelines for response, disclosing relevant information, engaging in meaningful discussion, responding to concerns raised in those discussions, and, in appropriate circumstances, accommodating Aboriginal interests.[11]

The principle that the government must act consistently with the honour of the Crown co-exists with a recognition of the principle that "the process itself would likely fall to be examined on a standard of reasonableness. Perfect satisfaction is not required."[12] The Federal Court of Appeal thus ruled in June 2008 in *Ahousaht Indian Band* v. *Canada (Minister of Fisheries & Oceans)* that "reasonable efforts to inform and consult . . . would normally suffice to discharge the duty."[13] This latter principle, how-

---

9   *Haida Nation, supra* note 1 at para. 43.

10   *Ibid.* at para. 41.

11   *Ibid.,* at paras. 43-45; *Taku River Tlingit First Nation* v. *British Columbia (Project Assessment Director)*, [2004] 3 S.C.R. 550, 2004 SCC 74 at para. 32.

12   *Haida Nation, ibid.* at para. 62.

13   *Ahousaht Indian Band* v. *Canada (Minister of Fisheries & Oceans)*, 2008 FCA 112 at para. 54. See *also Saulteau First Nation* v. *British Columbia (Oil and*

ever, does not mean that governments should be guided by anything less than honour. The content of the duty to consult is informed by honour, but the question is not whether the government achieves perfection but whether it acts reasonably and in good faith in attempting to pursue the aims of consultation.

The Supreme Court of Canada's case law provides the initial guidance on the spectrum of requirements within the duty to consult. In general terms, McLachlin C.J.C. explains in *Haida Nation*:

> The content of the duty to consult and accommodate varies with the circumstances. Precisely what duties arise in different situations will be defined as the case law in this emerging area develops. In general terms, however, it may be asserted that the scope of the duty is proportionate to a preliminary assessment of the strength of the case supporting the existence of the right or title, and to the seriousness of the potentially adverse effect upon the right or title claimed.[14]

This spectrum analysis, of course, differs in a significant manner in the treaty rights context as compared to the Aboriginal title or Aboriginal rights context. In the former, the existence of a particular right will typically already be clear, and appropriate consultation hinges pivotally on the seriousness of the potential impact on the treaty right. This is the point the Supreme Court of Canada makes clear in the *Mikisew Cree* case:

> In the case of a treaty the Crown, as a party, will always have notice of its contents. The question in each case will therefore be to determine the degree to which conduct contemplated by the Crown would adversely affect those rights so as to trigger the duty to consult. *Haida Nation* and *Taku River* set a low threshold. The flexibility lies not in the trigger ("might adversely affect it") but in the variable content of the duty once triggered.[15]

Gas Commission), 2004 BCCA 286 (adopting a reasonableness rather than a fiduciary standard on the Crown); leave to appeal to S.C.C. refused 30463 (3 Mar. 2005).

14 *Haida Nation*, *supra* note 1 at para. 39.

15 *Mikisew Cree First Nation* v. *Canada (Minister of Canadian Heritage)*, 2005 SCC 69, [2005] 3 S.C.R. 388 at para. 34.

In any event, there is a need for further clarification of the requirement of "meaningful consultation appropriate to the circumstances."[16] The Court suggests that the content of this requirement can be described appropriately in terms of a spectrum of requirements. Chief Justice McLachlin provides the Court's initial outline:

> At one end of the spectrum lie cases where the claim to title is weak, the Aboriginal right limited, or the potential for infringement minor. In such cases, the only duty on the Crown may be to give notice, disclose information, and discuss any issues raised in response to the notice. . . . At the other end of the spectrum lie cases where a strong *prima facie* case for the claim is established, the right and potential infringement is of high significance to the Aboriginal peoples, and the risk of non-compensable damage is high. In such cases deep consultation, aimed at finding a satisfactory interim solution, may be required. While precise requirements will vary with the circumstances, the consultation required at this stage may entail the opportunity to make submissions for consideration, formal participation in the decision-making process, and provision of written reasons to show that Aboriginal concerns were considered and to reveal the impact they had on the decision. This list is neither exhaustive, nor mandatory for every case. The government may wish to adopt dispute resolution procedures like mediation or administrative regimes with impartial decisionmakers in complex or difficult cases. . . . Between these two extremes of the spectrum just described, will lie other situations. Every case must be approached individually. Each must also be approached flexibly, since the level of consultation required may change as the process goes on and new information comes to light. The controlling question in all situations is what is required to maintain the honour of the Crown and to effect reconciliation between the Crown and the Aboriginal peoples with respect to the interests at stake.[17]

In the *Haida Nation* case itself, there was a strong *prima facie* claim to Aboriginal title, and the contemplated granting of tree farm licenses affected forests in a manner having potentially serious impacts on the Haida Na-

---

16   *Haida Nation, supra* note 1 at para. 41.

17   *Ibid.* at paras. 43-45.

tion, so the Court indicated that the duty to consult in the circumstances would be above the minimal level and, indeed, would likely extend to a degree of accommodation.[18]

Where there had been no consultation at all, the Crown had fallen short of its duty to consult. In the companion judgement in the *Taku River Tlingit First Nation* case,[19] the acceptance of the community's claim into treaty negotiations demonstrated the relative strength of its *prima facie* claims, and the potential effect on the community of proposed road construction was significant, so the Court again indicated that the content of the duty to consult in the circumstances would extend beyond the minimal requirements of notice, disclosure, and consultation to include what it termed a "level of responsiveness to [the community's] concerns."[20] In this case, however, the Court held that a process of consultations under the provincial *Environmental Assessment Act* had been sufficient to meet the requirements of the duty to consult as it offered meaningful opportunities for consultation and was leading toward accommodations within appropriate stages of the development of the project under consideration.[21]

In this latter case, the duty to consult with Aboriginal communities was fulfilled in the context of environmental assessment procedures; however, it was in the specific terms of an Aboriginal consultation process within the broader environmental assessment.[22] Some stakeholders in the resource industries have concerns about the potential consequences of Aboriginal law duty to consult practices becoming separate from other consultation processes; they are concerned that a consultation process that excludes other stakeholders may not meet the requirements of administrative law natural justice for others.[23]

At the same time, others have concerns with trying to fit Aboriginal

---

18 *Ibid.* at paras. 74, 77.

19 *Taku River Tlingit First Nation, supra* note 11.

20 *Ibid.* at para. 31.

21 *Ibid.* at paras. 33-46.

22 *Ibid.* at paras. 40-41.

23 See, for example, Bernie J. Roth, "Meeting the Expectations for Public Consultation Under Guide 56" (1 Oct. 2002, Fraser Milner Casgrain), www.fmclaw.com/upload/en/publications/archive/2612107_MeetingExpectations_Bernie_Roth.pdf, at 7-8.

consultation too directly into other processes,[24] for it is clear that the law will not inherently treat a simple public notice under an environmental consultation process as fulfilling requirements within the duty to consult Aboriginal communities[25] — although this conclusion depends on the position of particular circumstances on the spectrum analysis. In the specific circumstances of development on private land near a reserve, for instance, the requirements of the duty to consult may not include an enhanced right of notice but instead be met by the standard process of advertising and sending notice of a hearing on the matter.[26] The relationship of appropriate consultation with Aboriginal communities to other consultation processes mandated by administrative law principles or specific environmental assessment regimes will thus depend on specific circumstances.

There have often been assumptions that consultation with Aboriginal communities is necessarily a separate process from other public consultation. The constitutional origins of the duty to consult Aboriginal communities do give it a special status that cannot be attributed to all other consultation. However, at the same time, in at least some circumstances, it will be the case that a general public consultation process will simultaneously address at least some of the Aboriginal consultation required.[27] Thus, when a review panel on a pipeline carries out a broad public consultation that is open to Aboriginal representations as well, it may well be that its process at least partly fulfills the duty to consult, with whether it does so completely being dependent upon the degree to which that process meets the standard of the required meaningful consultation. And, indeed, there have been some instances in which Aboriginal communities have objected to being part of separate consultation processes rather than having a place in the main consultation process. On the other hand, many Aboriginal com-

---

24   I am grateful to my former colleague, Marie-Ann Bowden, for discussion on this issue.

25   See *Dene Tha' First Nation* v. *Canada (Minister of Environment)*, 2006 FC 1354, [2007] 1 C.N.L.R. 1 [*Dene Tha'* (Fed. Ct.)] at para. 62; deciding a public forum process was not sufficient to meet the requirements of consultation with the Dene Tha' First Nation; aff'd 2008 FCA 20, 378 N.R. 251.

26   See *Paul First Nation* v. *Parkland (County)*, 2006 ABCA 128, 384 A.R. 366, at paras. 2-3, 7, 15. There would obviously be an exception giving rise to enhanced notice requirements if there were knowledge of specific Aboriginal rights affected.

27   For an example, see *Taku River, supra* note 11.

munities do view a separate consultation process as an important reflection of the kind of nation-to-nation relationship that they see consultation as helping to embody.

The design of consultation processes can thus be complex. The complexity certainly increases when multiple Aboriginal communities are potentially involved in a particular consultation. In at least some parts of the country, tensions between First Nations and Métis communities concerning the fact that their rights claims compete to at least some extent have led governments to very clearly separate First Nations consultation from Métis consultation. Where different First Nations communities have competing claims, the result will also be increased complexity to the design of consultation processes. The real-world application of the neat statements of the Supreme Court of Canada will very often be much messier than the Court may have assumed in elaborating the doctrine. This fact is a reason for the Court to exercise some caution in what it does in ongoing development of the doctrine, particularly in continuing to leave room for governmental flexibility in process design.

To return to the main theme, the spectrum on the duty to consult arises from two principal factors: the strength of the Aboriginal claim, and the seriousness of the impact of contemplated government action on the interests underlying that claim. These two elements of the spectrum analysis track roughly the three elements within the triggering test: knowledge of the Aboriginal claim, and the possibility of contemplated government action having an adverse impact on underlying Aboriginal interests.[28] However, the trigger test and the spectrum analysis are distinct analyses and must each be approached carefully and independently.

Where these preconditions do not attain the relevant threshold levels discussed above, there is no content to the duty to consult and, indeed, no duty to consult.[29] At the other extreme, in circumstances with a strong Aboriginal claim and serious potential impacts on it, there would be a duty to consult the Aboriginal community and accommodate relevant Aboriginal interests. The first element in the spectrum test, the *prima facie* strength of the claim for Aboriginal title, an Aboriginal right, or a treaty right actually falls to be determined to a degree based on jurisprudence from other areas of Aboriginal law and the evidence that fits those requirements. It is juris-

---

28   *Haida Nation, supra* note 1 at para. 35.

29   *R. v. Douglas*, 2007 BCCA 265, 278 D.L.R. (4th) 263, at paras. 42-44.

prudence on Aboriginal title claims, Aboriginal rights claims, and treaty rights claims that speaks to the strength of the relevant claims for a duty to consult and evidence of those underlying claims that affects the *prima facie* strength element.

The criterion concerning the strength of the claim raises certain complications. Frequently, all the relevant evidence is not immediately available to those assessing the *prima facie* strength of the Aboriginal claim. A government department considering the content of the duty to consult in particular circumstances may need to seek information from other departments with more specific knowledge of the particular claim. Even then, however, governments may well be operating without knowledge of all the specific evidence that an Aboriginal community may be able to present, such as the content of elders' testimony that may not be known to others. Nonetheless, a rough estimate of the *prima facie* strength of the claim may well flow reasonably from a preliminary assessment of known evidence concerning the connection of the claim to traditional territories and practices, from a comparison of the claim to other kinds of claims that have been successful or unsuccessful, and from a basic estimation of the likely success of a particular kind of claim.

Several issues are worthy of discussion in terms of their relationship to this dimension of the spectrum analysis. First, there is an element of shared responsibility over the identification of the rights claim and its assessment. On the one hand, the Crown has an obligation to attempt to identify the relevant rights claims; in a case where the federal Department of Transport did not conceive a claim correctly, the courts were ready to conclude that this made its resulting process of consultation unreasonable.[30] On the other hand, once notified of government action, Aboriginal communities have a responsibility to identify rights claims potentially affected; failure to do so may preclude further consultation requirements.[31] Thus, the Crown has a responsibility to identify accurately whether a duty to consult is triggered; thereafter, there is a shared responsibility through the initial phases of consultation to identify what is at stake so that appropriate further consultation or accommodation can be implemented.

Also in relation to this criterion, a difficult situation arises when more

30 *Metlakatla Indian Band* v. *Canada (Minister of Transport)*, 2007 FC 553, 65 Admin. L.R. (4th) 152 at para. 29.

31 See *Douglas, supra* note 29 at para. 161 and *Ahousaht Indian Band, supra* note 13 at paras. 52-53.

than one Aboriginal community has made a claim to title or a right that cannot be shared. The British Columbia Environmental Appeal Board dealt with such a situation in a decision involving the Xats'ull First Nation appealing a permit issued for the discharge of contaminants from a mining operation on the basis of an alleged failure to consult,[32] and the Environmental Appeal Board suggested that the Aboriginal title claim of the Xats'ull was weaker in parts of the claimed territory where their claim overlapped with those of other First Nations.[33] This was particularly problematic for the Xats'ull, as the areas closest to the discharge point and thus most likely to be affected by it were the areas where their title claim was now weakest.[34] The presence of overlapping claims has also been argued as a factor in the context of other duty to consult litigation.[35] Where there are overlapping claims, it would appear to weaken the probability of each Aboriginal community being successful in its claim, and it thus becomes something, according to the doctrine, that lessens the content of the duty to consult *vis-à-vis* each potentially affected Aboriginal community. This factor within the duty to consult analysis may be one additional reason for Aboriginal communities to seek to come to agreement on the extent of their respective claims.

The second element in the spectrum test is the seriousness of the impact of contemplated government action on the affected Aboriginal community. This has not attracted as much case law on complicating elements, but it would be fair to say that an important factor will be whether government action has potentially irreversible effects as opposed to more transitory ones.[36] In the case of potentially irreversible effects on vital Aboriginal interests, the expected degree of consultation — and quite possibly accommodation — will be high.[37] Furthermore, the kind of Aboriginal

---

32   *Xats'ull First Nation* v. *Director, Environmental Management Act*, 2006-EMA-006(a): www.eab.gov.bc.ca/ema/2006ema006a.pdf.

33   *Ibid.* at paras. 275, 279.

34   *Ibid.* at paras. 280-84, 302-304.

35   See , for example, *Musqueam Indian Band* v. *Canada,* 2008 FCA 214, [2008] 3 C.N.L.R. 29, at para. 8.

36   *Ka'a'gee Tu First Nation* v. *Canada (Minister of Indian & Northern Affairs),* 2007 FC 764, [2008] 2 F.C.R. 473.

37   See, for example, *Dene Tha'* (Fed. Ct.), *supra* note 25 at paras. 113, 114, 121; see also *Kwikwetlem First Nation* v. *British Columbia (Utilities Commission),* 2009 BCCA 68 at para. 70.

interest at stake may affect the assessment of the seriousness of the impact: a government impact on an economic interest will possibly attract a lesser consultation requirement within the spectrum than a government impact on certain kinds of cultural interests. This latter hypothesis flows from a consideration of the purposes of the doctrine. It is designed to protect Aboriginal and treaty rights for the sake of the ongoing life and vitality of Indigenous communities. That broad purpose of the doctrine can enable some identification and distinction of different kinds of effects as between less and more serious impacts.

These two factors of the *prima facie* strength of the Aboriginal or treaty rights claim and the potential seriousness of the government impact on the Aboriginal or treaty right at issue together determine where on the *Haida Nation* spectrum the duty to consult rests. Pursuant to this framework, varying possibilities then emerge for the content of the duty to consult in particular circumstances. It may range from minimal notice, disclosure, and responsiveness through to deep consultation that follows more complex administrative law approaches, seeks to develop interim solutions, and potentially makes use of appropriate dispute resolution procedures. On the one hand, the Supreme Court of Canada case law describes the application of these different requirements in terms of the application of the factors of the spectrum analysis. On the other, it roots them in the more principled but also more general analysis of what will best maintain the honour of the Crown and further the ends of reconciliation. As discussed in Chapter 1, these latter principles may not actually point in a single direction but in various directions. Because the spectrum serves only as a shorthand for the underlying purposes, the determination of the content of the duty to consult in particular circumstances remains as much art as science.

Recognizing that the spectrum established in *Haida Nation* and in judicial comments about it is not an all-determinative test is actually necessary to making sense of both the actual practice of consultation on-the-ground and of the possibility of different ways of reaching a determination as to the content of the duty to consult in particular circumstances. The key criterion is what makes for a meaningful consultation. Some governments have ended up using factors different than the *Haida Nation* factors themselves in different sorts of consultation matrices. Some Aboriginal communities have contemplated using different factors in their own consultation policies. Creativity is entirely possible in developing analyses of the appropriate kind of consultation for consultation to be meaningful in particular circumstances.

Something like particularly unique or complex environmental factors in a certain setting may also impact on the identification of meaningful consultation. For example, the unique environmental characteristics of the Arctic may call for the use of different factors in identifying appropriate depths of consultation in Arctic settings.[38]

The goal of consultation in each instance is an engagement by the Crown with Aboriginal communities in the manner necessary to make the duty to consult a meaningful enactment of its underlying goals. This can be seen through various factors in the consultation requirements, including the time for consultation, the expectations of the notice to the Aboriginal consultation partner, the opportunities offered for responses from the Aboriginal consultation partner, and the duty of accommodation where appropriate. Analyzing each element in terms of what makes the consultation meaningful helps to define the content of that element.

For example, the duty to consult in particular circumstances may well apply over a significant period of time and not be fulfilled through a one-off consultation. What determines this is what is necessary to the appropriate consultation requirements given where one is on the spectrum and what is responsive, ultimately, to the underlying purposes of the doctrine. Where it is important to the meaningfulness of the expected level of consultation, it may be essential for the Aboriginal consultation partner(s) to be engaged from the beginning and/or involved through to the end. An example of the former arises in the *Dene Tha'* case, in which the Federal Court held that the meaningfulness of consultation was undermined by the fact that the Dene Tha' had not been engaged in consultation from the beginning of planning on a pipeline that was to pass through their traditional territory.[39] An example of the latter arises in *Ka'a'gee Tu First Nation v. Canada (Indian Affairs and Northern Development)*[40] in which the Federal Court held that there had been a breach of the constitutional duty to consult because, although the Ka'a'gee Tu had had the chance to participate in some consultations, there was a final stage of decision-making with different elements under consideration in which they had no opportunity to be consulted. What is at issue in each case is when involvement in consul-

---

38   See Dwight Newman, Michelle Biddulph, & Lorelle Binnion, "Arctic Energy Development and Best Practices on Consultation with Indigenous Peoples" (2014) 32 Boston U. Int'l L.J. (forthcoming).

39   *Dene Tha'* (Fed. Ct.), *supra* note 25.

40   *Ka'a'gee Tu First Nation, supra* note 36.

tation is meaningful, and the courts have repeatedly drawn on this concept of what timeline makes consultation "meaningful."[41]

Obviously, the timeline of when consultation must begin relates back to the triggering questions discussed in the previous chapter. There is a danger in looking at a course of government action in retrospect, in that one can come to the view that consultation should have been present from the beginning based on later consequences that were not identified at the first moment, such as where government awareness was reasonably limited or where the government's contemplated action evolved over the course of the project. This imposes an impossible standard on governments. That being said, there is also a danger in not identifying the full scope of what is under contemplation. The duty to consult test calls for careful analysis in light of its purposes.

In terms of notice to an Aboriginal consultation partner, it is clear that an overly short comment period may undermine the effect of a notice, and that a notice must be directed specifically to an Aboriginal community — as opposed to, as in one case, simply being posted on the Internet for whoever happens to come across it.[42] Again, what is important is that which will further meaningful consultation — meaningful in terms of responding to the goals of entering into the consultation process in the first place. Thinking of the content of the duty to consult in these terms, of course, makes crucial how we understand the duty to consult in theoretical terms, such as in the models raised in Chapter 1. What makes consultation meaningful under one model may differ under another. But the fundamental parameters on a consultation call, at a minimum, for appropriate timing, appropriate notice, and a meaningful opportunity to respond.

The concept of meaningfulness is not a concept requiring maximal consultation in every instance. To think in that way would be to think inconsistently with the Supreme Court of Canada's use of the spectrum analysis in the first place. The concept of meaningful consultation is not inconsistent, for example, with scaling the depth of consultation to the scale of a particular project and thus ensuring that consultation is economically manageable in the context of different projects. Doing so may well be essential to consultation working as a living practice.

---

41   See, for example, *Dene Tha'* (Fed. Ct.), *supra* note 25 at paras. 113, 114, 121; see also *Kwikwetlem First Nation, supra* note 37 at para. 70.

42   *Dene Tha'* (Fed. Ct.), *supra* note 25 at para. 116. Cf. also *Beckman* v. *Little Salmon/Carmacks First Nation*, 2010 SCC 53, [2010] 3 S.C.R. 103 at para. 33.

Different provinces will actually face quite different issues around consultation. For example, consultation in Saskatchewan operates in a different context than it does in British Columbia. A Saskatchewan consultation will frequently pertain to treaty rights rather than any other Aboriginal right, and Aboriginal title claims have very limited application, if any, in the Saskatchewan context. There are, for example, ongoing issues about whether the Dakota Sioux, who did not have a treaty relationship because they were possibly an American Aboriginal community that moved to Canada (although this narrative is contested), might have any kind of Aboriginal title claim at all. The result is that the *prima facie* strength of an Aboriginal claim will typically not be a distinguishing factor in different circumstances — although the strength of different treaty interpretations sometimes will be — leaving the seriousness of impact on the relevant Aboriginal interests the key distinguishing factor set out in the case law in this treaty rights context.[43] By contrast, many of the issues in British Columbia will be Aboriginal rights or Aboriginal title questions, but with the *prima facie* strength of those claims very much at issue in different parts of the province. In that setting, both the impact on the community and the *prima facie* strength of its claims will operate as full factors in helping to identify meaningful consultation.

On the spectrum analysis, the deepest consultation is required when there is both a strong *prima facie* claim and a major potential impact, a much more limited consultation when there is a weak *prima facie* claim and little potential impact, and a moderate level of consultation in the intermediate cases. But what is at stake in every context is meaningful consultation, appropriate to the complex set of circumstances.

An example of how a court approaches matters may help clarify the content of the duty to consult. The May 2009 judgement of the Federal Court in *Brokenhead Ojibway Nation* v. *Canada (Attorney General)*[44] is an example of a case that was closely watched as testing the implications of the duty to consult in the context of a set of pipeline projects, one of which was the Keystone Pipeline, by which name it has become known. Just what approach the courts take to the duty to consult in this case arguably has significant implications for other resource development projects, notably

---

43   Cf. *Mikisew Cree First Nation, supra* note 15 at paras. 55-57, discussing the role of the seriousness of impact on the Aboriginal community as foremost in a treaty context.

44   *Brokenhead Ojibway Nation* v. *Canada (Attorney General)*, 2009 FC 484.

other pipeline projects.

In the *Brokenhead Ojibway* case, the seven First Nations seeking declaratory relief against the pipelines running through their traditional lands in southern Manitoba asserted that there had been inadequate consultation. Officials to whom they had written had not engaged with them. The Prime Minister, the Minister of Indian Affairs, other ministers, and the Secretary of the Governor in Council (GIC) had apparently not even acknowledged their correspondence.[45] Their concerns related both to the site-specific impacts of the projects, many of which were considered in National Energy Board proceedings, and broader concerns about the impact of the pipelines on future treaty land claims or the spiritual relation of First Nations to their traditional territories. The Attorney General of Canada argued that consultation had taken place through the engagement of corporate entities with the First Nations and the National Energy Board — in effect, holding that the Board's conduct of its role helped fulfill the duty to consult. Significantly, Barnes J. in the Federal Court judgement of May 2009 held that the use of existing regulatory processes may satisfy the duty to consult, depending on the overriding responsibility of the Crown to ensure the adequacy of these processes in the circumstances at issue.[46] This latter point is significant, for it implies that there could effectively be, in some contexts, an obligation to enhance regulatory processes, at least if they are meant to be relied upon as playing a part in consultation.

In the judgement, Barnes J. emphasizes "the principle that the content of the duty to consult with First Nations is proportionate to both the potential strength of the claim or right asserted and the anticipated impact of a development or project on these asserted interests."[47] This invocation of the spectrum analysis situates the case within the overall legal framework of the content of the duty to consult. Evidence of extensive engagement around site-specific concerns and the National Energy Board's ability to scrutinize those site-specific arrangements went far in convincing Barnes J. that there had been appropriate consultation in some respects.[48] Possible concerns remained if there were more overarching rights threatened. However, Barnes J. emphasized that "[t]here must be some unresolved

---

45   *Ibid.* at para. 20.

46   *Ibid.* at para. 25.

47   *Ibid.* at para. 23.

48   *Ibid.* at para. 26.

non-negligible impact arising from such a development to engage the Crown's duty to consult."[49] This statement may appear to refer to the triggering of the duty, but the point, rather, is that there may be a stronger duty to consult in relation to site-specific impacts and less or no duty to consult on broader matters where there is not a sufficiently strong impact demonstrated on other rights. The content of the duty to consult can vary even within the context of a single project or issue, with stronger content to the duty in some respects than in others. In this case, Barnes J. seeks to distinguish the demonstrated impact from that in other cases[50] and notes that the pipeline projects are largely on private land — land that had been previously developed and was not readily susceptible of treaty rights claims in any event.[51]

What is interesting here is not solely the conclusion but also the analysis. The analysis is based on a careful application of the spectrum analysis within a specific factual context; this analysis can involve comparisons to other cases and even the drawing of distinctions between different potential forms of consultation in the case at hand. When Barnes J. concludes that any duty to consult was met by the proceedings of the National Energy Board and the opportunities it offered for consultation and accommodation, the decision is geared to analyzing how potential impacts on Aboriginal and treaty rights needed to be considered in light of the impacts at issue.

As suggested at the outset of discussing this case, it likely has major significance for other pipeline projects, whether the Mackenzie Valley Pipeline (if it ever regains momentum) or the Northern Gateway Pipeline, although other situations will obviously fall ultimately to be tested on their own facts and processes. And, indeed, there are differences given the shape of the doctrine, notably as between pipeline projects that use existing rights-of-way as opposed to those that involve new construction. On this latter point, in particular, a pipeline project that uses existing rights-of-way (or, as in the *Brokenhead Ojibway* case, simply uses private lands) begins with a major advantage in that any historical breaches of Aboriginal or treaty rights when those rights-of-way were created do not now become issues. With a new pipeline project using new rights-of-way on previously

---

49   *Ibid.* at para. 34.

50   *Ibid.* at paras. 39-41.

51   *Ibid.* at para. 30.

Crown lands, every uncertainty concerning possible Aboriginal or treaty rights gets put onto the duty to consult table.

However, even in this latter situation, which might make it look like the duty to consult doctrine poses an insurmountable obstacle to the transportation infrastructure needed by an energy superpower like Canada, the *Brokenhead Ojibway* analysis actually has significant lessons concerning the fact that processes can be designed that attempt to find a path that balances the claims of different Aboriginal communities along a lengthy pipeline route. Where some Aboriginal communities are supportive of a project and others are opposed, there can be an appropriate process that gets at the duty to consult issues that are at stake but that does not necessarily impede a project based simply on the presence of complex and sometimes competing considerations. The question is always whether there is, through a contextually appropriate process, meaningful consultation.

The content of the duty to consult in any given case will be contextual and fact-specific, albeit within the broad framework this chapter has outlined in terms of the spectrum analysis and the fundamental components of meaningful consultation: notice and appropriate timelines for response, appropriate disclosure of relevant information, discussion appropriate to the circumstances, responding to concerns raised in discussions, and potentially accommodating concerns in appropriate circumstances. It is to some of the broader questions around accommodation that we now turn.

3.3 Duties of Accommodation

The Supreme Court of Canada's decision in *Haida Nation* makes clear that accommodation will not always be required in the context of consultation, but indicates that it will sometimes be required as a component of the duty to consult. Chief Justice McLachlin describes these principles:

[T]he effect of good faith consultation may be to reveal a duty to accommodate. Where a strong *prima facie* case exists for the claim, and the consequences of the government's proposed decision may adversely affect it in a significant way, addressing the Aboriginal concerns may require taking steps to avoid irreparable harm or to minimize the effects of infringement, pending final resolution of the underlying claim.[52]

Any such accommodation will be developed in the context of complex competing interests, with McLachlin C.J.C. going on to write:

> Balance and compromise are inherent in the notion of reconciliation. Where accommodation is required in making decisions that may adversely affect as yet unproven Aboriginal rights and title claims, the Crown must balance Aboriginal concerns reasonably with the potential impact of the decision on the asserted right or title and with other societal interests.[53]

The language here is quite open-textured, and other cases have done little to define further the requirements of accommodation. Industry stakeholders consulted during the writing of this book identified uncertainty about the legal requirements in terms of accommodation as one of the most vexing dimensions of the duty to consult doctrine. To this point, accommodation is described in the case law simply in terms of what interim arrangements will avoid irreparable effects on Aboriginal interests and what interim arrangements will minimize harm to Aboriginal interests, all in the context of the underlying aims of the duty to consult doctrine.[54]

The emphasis on the aims of the duty to consult doctrine is an important guiding principle. In the *Dene Tha'* case, for instance, Phelan J. emphasized that consultation should be geared to reconciliation and, indeed, suggested that the "goal of consultation is not to be narrowly interpreted as the mitigation of adverse effects on Aboriginal rights and/or title."[55] This nuance provides an example of where the different theoretical perspectives one could take to the duty to consult have different implications for a fundamental matter like the accommodations implied. These principles admittedly leave much undecided to this point, and there is much room for the case law to develop in this area. Interestingly, to date, the cases that have ended up in litigation have tended to be more about whether there was a recognition of the need for consultation or an adequate effort at consulta-

---

52 *Haida Nation, supra* note 1 at para. 47.

53 *Ibid.* at para. 50.

54 *Haida Nation* provides that minimal guidance in *ibid.* at para. 47.

55 *Dene Tha'* (Fed. Ct.), *supra* note 25 at para. 82.

tion rather than whether there was an appropriate accommodation of interests identified through well-functioning consultations. This may mean that governments have made good faith efforts when Aboriginal interests were identified, thus avoiding litigation. But it is also something on which there could be ongoing development in future.

Any accommodations arising from consultations are going to be fact-specific. They ought to be oriented to the principles behind the duty to consult and advance these principles in a reasonable way. The debates around these principles need not postpone practical action. Where one routing of a proposed road has a significant impact on an Aboriginal community's interests, and it is reasonably possible to reroute the road, doing so will both minimize the impact on the Aboriginal community and further the reconciliation of diverse communities in the Canadian federation. Some accommodations will simply amount to practical adjustments to plans such that they are taking account of Aboriginal interests in a reasonable manner. The tougher questions arise in circumstances where the necessary adjustments would come at a high cost, particularly those that would make a project no longer viable. In those circumstances, there must be a weighing of the different interests with an openness to talking them through. No doctrine can make for easy choices.

Sometimes, those within Aboriginal communities who are more skeptical of the goals of the courts suggest that the duty to consult doctrine does not mean anything because governments can go ahead with approvals of projects right away after carrying out their consultation exercises. At an academic level, UBC law professor Gordon Christie has come close to putting that sort of view.[56] However, experience over the years with the doctrine does show that it can lead to major modifications to projects or even cancellations of projects that would have unacceptably severe impacts on Aboriginal communities.

An example of a project where accommodation of Aboriginal interests led to cancellation of the project is arguably present in the context of the decision not to permit Taseko to proceed with its Prosperity Mine project in British Columbia. Two different proposals put by Taseko were both found to be likely to lead to significant impacts on a lake that was of spiritual significance to a local Aboriginal community. Although separating the

---

56   Gordon Christie, "A Colonial Reading of Recent Jurisprudence: Sparrow, Delgamuukw and Haida Nation" (2005) 23 *Windsor Yearbook of Access to Justice* 17.

environmental dimensions of these impacts and their spiritual significance to the Aboriginal community is not possible, the record of what occurred suggests that the federal government gave careful consideration to factors that included the impacts on the Aboriginal community. The first proposal received provincial approval but was sent back for redesign by the federal Cabinet. Taseko returned with another proposal, but the ongoing presence in the proposal of impacts on the spiritually significant lake continued to pose problems, and the federal government rejected this new proposal in February 2014. Aboriginal rights articulated through consultation thus led to the cancellation of a major mining project. The example does not say that Aboriginal rights will always block development, nor that Aboriginal communities will even wish always to block development, but in the context of particularly severe impacts on an Aboriginal community's underlying cultural and spiritual values, there will be instances where consultation contributes to the cancellation of a major project, even a multi-billion dollar mine.

3.4 Economic Accommodation

One particularly uncertain element of accommodation relates to so-called "economic accommodation." Where judges have engaged directly with duty to consult situations that potentially raise "economic accommodation" as one of the matters at issue, they have been circumspect. The implications of any decision, obviously, are significant because of the possible precedent for other situations. Justice Neilson acknowledged as much in her decision in the *Wii'litswx* case:

> Turning to Gitanyow's interest in revenue sharing, the economic component of aboriginal interests is clearly a significant issue, with wide-ranging repercussions for all citizens of British Columbia. In my view, in the course of balancing Gitanyow's interests against other societal interests, the Crown may be justifiably wary of dealing with revenue sharing on an individualized basis. For example, I do not find it unreasonable for the Crown to decline to consider Gitanyow's claim for substantial sums as its share of past and future logging revenue until the ramifications of such an approach can be considered at a broader level. I am satisfied that, in the interim, the periodic payments made by the Crown to support ongoing initiatives, and the

development of a consultation framework to consider alternative means of accommodating the economic aspects of aboriginal interests, suggest good faith, ongoing consultation and accommodation on the part of the Crown to advance this process. It is regrettable that this initiative appears to be moving at such a slow pace, but at present it apparently has the blessing of both the Crown and the First Nations Forest Council.[57]

Acknowledging that there are many uncertainties remaining, it is nonetheless possible to comment on differing possibilities for economic accommodation in different places. British Columbia's lack of historical treaties means that much of the province is subject to Aboriginal title claims. Effects on Aboriginal title will almost invariably give rise to claims for economic accommodation because Aboriginal title is an interest in land which, while *sui generis*, is more analogous to fee simple than other interests arising from Aboriginal rights[58] and has what the courts have sometimes called an "inescapable economic component."[59] Where the scope of the duty to consult concerns consultation around the content of treaty rights, such as in Saskatchewan, the role of economic accommodation is not as clear. Aboriginal communities have certainly asserted that their understanding of the spirit of the treaties would give rise to a role for economic accommodation and resource revenue-sharing.[60] Governments have a different perspective on this, and there are very complex considerations that arise.

As stated, British Columbia is, in some ways, the province the most affected by these questions of accommodation. Much of the province remains subject to unresolved treaty claims, and the presence of Aboriginal title claims, in particular, gives rise to the possibility of economic accommodation being an appropriate response to the possible infringements on asserted rights arising from resource development. As an interim measure, economic accommodation has thus developed in at least certain contexts in British Columbia. In particular, the province of British Columbia has

---

57   *Wii'litswx* v. *British Columbia (Minister of Forests)*, 2008 BCSC 1139, [2008] 4 C.N.L.R. 315, at para. 239.

58   *Delgamuukw* v. *British Columbia* [1997] 3 S.C.R. 1010 at para. 111.

59   *Ibid.* at para. 166.

60   See, for example, James Wood, "Resource Revenues Key: FSIN," *Saskatoon StarPhoenix* (27 Jan. 2009) A3.

some ninety Forest Consultation and Revenue Sharing Agreements, with the first of these having been signed in December 2010.[61] The texts of these agreements provide for interim economic accommodation, often in the form of specific annual sums to be paid from the government's forestry royalties to the particular First Nation.[62] Some other agreements, however, include percentage shares of resource revenues as opposed simply to flat sums. The *McLeod Lake Indian Band Economic and Community Development Agreement* of 25 August 2010 provides for 15 per cent of *Mineral Act* taxes paid by mine proponents for developments in the McLeod Lake traditional territory to be paid over to the community.[63] Some other agreements provide for different shares. For example, the Stk̓emlúpsemc of the *Scwempemc Nation Economic and Community Development Agreement*, signed the day prior to the McLeod Lake agreement, provides for a 37.5 per cent share of *Mineral Act* taxes from that community's traditional territory.[64]

These latter examples, and the differing arrangements with different Aboriginal communities, illustrate some challenges that may emerge in the context of economic accommodation arrangements. There may be very good reasons for the differences in the payment arrangements. These differences may originate, for example, in the different *prima facie* strength of the different Aboriginal communities' claims, which might reasonably lead to a different accommodation of uncertainty in the different situations. However, some differences could conceivably originate from other factors, such as different negotiating tactics of different communities, rather than from pure legal considerations.

Moreover, whatever the underlying reasons, there are apt to be at least differing perceptions on the fairness of the different shares garnered by different communities. Although the issue has not yet garnered much attention, a whole set of major policy questions may arise in the coming years

---

61   For a list, see *Forest Consultation and Revenue Sharing Agreements*: www. newrelationship.gov.bc.ca.

62   For just one example, see *Sia'new First Nation Forest & Range Consultation and Revenue Sharing Agreement* of 11 March 2013, s. 3.2, available online, *ibid.*

63   *McLeod Lake Indian Band Economic and Community Development Agreement* of 25 August 2010, s. 3.1(c), available online, *ibid.*

64   *Stk̓emlúpsemc of the Scwempemc Nation Economic and Community Development Agreement* of 24 August 2010, s. 3.1(c), available online, *ibid.*

from a developing reality that, through a combination of differing natural resource endowments on traditional territories and differing legal relationships concerning those territories, different Aboriginal communities in Canada will be endowed with very different amounts of natural resource wealth. Some communities are now already positioned for vast amounts of resource wealth, whereas others are much less likely to benefit. That reality may lead to very different dynamics in Aboriginal politics and consideration of different Aboriginal law issues compared to times when Aboriginal communities were economically disadvantaged but at least equally disadvantaged across different communities.

Provinces other than British Columbia have also seriously contemplated the development of different types of resource revenue sharing arrangements. For example, Ontario has been engaged in related discussions over recent years. Some of the contemplated arrangements have involved arrangements that would involve equalization formulae on resource revenues as between different Aboriginal communities as opposed simply to individualized deals with specific communities. However, there has not been any resolution as to an arrangement, and Aboriginal communities have pressed for much larger sums than the Ontario government has been ready to offer. At one stage in late 2012, a group of First Nation leaders from northwestern Ontario were pressing for a substantial payment for past resource extraction and were citing a study produced by a business professor to support them in claiming $32 billion.[65]

Such sums are clearly beyond governmental contemplation. But they point to the magnitude of what is at stake. Moreover, if some Aboriginal communities with fortunate geographies for natural resources claim such sums, questions will certainly arise as to distributions with other communities. Nobody should underestimate the ongoing challenges and the magnitude of the questions that Canada faces.

From a policy point of view, there are many questions to ask in terms of what it is that resource revenue deals are meant to further. There are questions to ask in terms of what kind of policies will best promote future economic activity and success within Aboriginal communities, which might best be thought of in terms of policies that build businesses and employment more so than those that simply provide "compensation." There are

---

65   See Ian Ross, "Resource Revenue Sharing a Thorny Issue for Ontario," *Northern Ontario Business* (8 September 2012).

questions to be asked about fairness as between different Aboriginal communities and as between Aboriginal communities and others. There are questions to be asked about whether resource revenue shares are a stable source of funds for Aboriginal communities or if they actually represent an undesirably volatile revenue stream.[66]

Severe dangers exist that political processes are not always appropriately oriented for these kinds of questions. Attempts to deal with such questions in the context of election-cycle politics can produce all kinds of difficulties. They may make revenue sharing arrangements beyond contemplation. They may also lead some parties to propose particular revenue sharing arrangements that have not been the subject of good policy design but that are instead catering to particular political constituencies. For example, during the 2011 Saskatchewan election campaign, an opposition party facing desperate political circumstances proposed resource revenue sharing as a campaign promise in circumstances that looked much like the party was catering to political forces literally in one electoral constituency that it hoped to win. The promise offered resource revenue sharing for First Nations only and excluded Métis communities. And it was seen by many as a divisive political manoeuvre.[67] The questions about good policy in this area are important. So are those about what will or will not promote good relations between Aboriginal and non-Aboriginal Canadians.

Apart from broader thinking about economic accommodation, some case law has admittedly referred to the possibility of compensation for a breach of the duty to consult once that breach is a *fait accompli,* and reversing a course of action to enforce the duty to consult is no longer viable.[68] In certain limited circumstances, compensation may flow from past acts or be a form of economic accommodation. However, courts may or may not be ready to award compensation for far-reaching retroactive claims, such as those that the Beaver Lake Cree Nation has attempted to put for lack of past consultation in relation to tens of thousands of oil and gas permits on

---

66   I presented some such considerations at the University of Toronto's 35@30 Conference in October 2012 in a paper entitled "Consultation and Economic Reconciliation" that will be forthcoming in a book stemming from the conference to be edited by Patrick Macklem and Douglas Sanderson.

67   I wrote an op-ed against the proposal: Dwight Newman, "Revenue Sharing Proposal Divisive, Unwise," *Saskatoon StarPhoenix* (27 October 2011).

68   See *Hupacasath First Nation* v. *British Columbia (Minister of Forests),* 2008 BCSC 1505, [2009] 1 C.N.L.R. 30 at paras. 231-32.

its traditional territory reaching back to the mid-1990s. In the context of the Beaver Lake Cree Nation's claim, the latest decision after various procedural points has been an Alberta Court of Appeal decision not to strike out the litigation, with the Court urging the development of a plan to get the litigation to trial on its merits.[69] Time will tell what comes from it, if anything. Apart from governmental policies in relation to resource revenue sharing, the decisions of courts in such cases may have major implications for the duty to consult, and, indeed, for relations between Aboriginal and non-Aboriginal Canadians for years, decades, and centuries to come.

Ongoing discussions around economic accommodation will shape significantly what the duty to consult means in pragmatic terms. Revenue-sharing may be appropriate in some circumstances, particularly where Aboriginal communities hold a right that has economic dimensions, such as Aboriginal title. Even in circumstances where it is not legally required, governments will no doubt consider the possibility, not least because of potential inequalities arising between different Aboriginal communities if some are excluded from economic accommodation because of the happenstance of history. However, economic accommodation may take place in ways other than revenue-sharing, and these may include other impact benefit arrangements that further the interests of various parties. What will be necessary is to continue working toward relationships of trust that give rise to reasonable arrangements that can be accepted on all sides and that achieve good policy goals. As aptly put by Southin J.A. of the British Columbia Court of Appeal,

> [t]he core of accommodation is the balancing of interests and the reaching of a compromise until such time as claimed rights to property are finally resolved. In relatively undeveloped areas of the province, I should think accommodation might take a multiplicity of forms such as a sharing of mineral or timber resources. One could also envisage employment agreements or land transfers and the like. This is a developing area of the law and it is too early to be at all categorical about the ambit of appropriate accommodative solutions that have to work not only for First Nations people but for all of the populace having a broad regard to the public interest.[70]

---

69   See *Lameman* v. *Alberta*, 2013 ABCA 148, 85 Alta. L. Rev. (5th) 64.

70   *Musqueam Indian Band* v. *British Columbia (Minister of Sustainable Resource*

The design of appropriate approaches that respect the full public interest will be one of the great challenges in the context of claims to economic accommodation. There is very significant work to do in the years ahead to consider and appropriately approach these questions in a way that genuinely respects all sides of some very complex issues.

3.5 Leveraging the Duty to Consult

Some communities are not enthusiastic simply to wait for grand schemes of revenue sharing but are looking, rather, to develop tangible ways to draw upon the duty to consult doctrine so as to promote economic activity now. In important ways, the duty to consult can already function as a lever for deals between private industry stakeholders and Aboriginal communities. In particular, industry stakeholders may be enthusiastic to eliminate future legal risks. The duty to consult represents a set of risks in relation to resource projects on Aboriginal communities' traditional territories. Thus, it is not uncommon, as described in Chapter 2, for industry stakeholders to find ways to, in effect, negotiate around the duty to consult. Aboriginal communities that wish to clarify parameters around development, to welcome some development, and to stop development that harms vital interests, are seeking to find ways to leverage the duty to consult doctrine into win-win relationships.

One means by which some Aboriginal communities are establishing parameters on development — protecting vitally important areas within their traditional territories while making clearer where development is possible and welcome — is through the development of different forms of Indigenous land use surveys. One particularly prominent methodology is that employed by Terry Tobias, who recently published a major book on the topic.[71] The maps produced draw upon oral history and interviewing, and they then depict the geographical usage of various areas within a reserve or traditional territory in a manner such that it becomes easier to identify potential impacts from contemplated development and to then consider how to address those impacts. Some Aboriginal communities will feel less comfortable with establishing such maps, particularly if they in some manner

---

Management), 2005 BCCA 128, 251 D.L.R. (4th) 717 at para. 98.

71   Terry N. Tobias, *Living Proof: The Essential Data-Collection-Guide for Indigenous Use-and-Occupancy Map Surveys* (Vancouver: Ecotrust Canada & Union of British Columbia Indian Chiefs, 2009).

reveal information that was traditionally secret knowledge. However, even those latter concerns may be something that can be addressed through appropriate confidentiality agreements, at least depending upon local traditions concerning the sharing of that secret knowledge and whether means can be developed in a modern context for carefully limited exceptions to traditional rules on that knowledge.

An Aboriginal community that is ready to engage proactively with an industry stakeholder that is ready to develop relationships with that community can help to shape development in a manner meeting community interests by being at least somewhat forthcoming with a readiness to engage on what interests are core and cannot be touched and what interests are subject to the negotiation of different arrangements. In doing so, the community may find paths forward to negotiated agreements that go around the legal technicalities of the duty to consult but that fundamentally leverage the doctrine into win-win arrangements for all.

The fact that individual communities can do so in light of the doctrine as it has developed to date may actually accentuate the public policy challenges that emerge in the context of the doctrine. The reality is that some individual communities that were well positioned to do so have already struck deals that include very significant sums of money. These communities will likely not be enthusiastic to surrender these arrangements for the sake of equalization with other Aboriginal communities. There may already be a pattern developing in which some Aboriginal communities will in fact have massive resource wealth and business advantages over others, which will put various strains on the policy and legal framework around Aboriginal issues in the years and decades ahead. Those interested in Aboriginal issues in Canada can, on the one hand, welcome economic development that has grown from the duty to consult. At the same time, they must realize that there will be new issues ahead and a need for ongoing study and thought on these issues.

3.6 Rising Above the Minimum Legal Requirements

A legally acceptable consultation, as discussed in these past two chapters, must meet the basic criterion of meaningfulness. It must be initiated at an appropriate stage. There must be an identification of the Aboriginal communities potentially affected and an identification of contact people among those communities. There must be appropriate forms of notice given and further information made available where necessary for meaningful con-sultation. In cases of deeper consultation, it will be necessary to convene meetings to discuss the concerns that are arising. In any case, it is necessary to have lines of communication genuinely open to hear the implications of Aboriginal interests. In cases where accommodation issues arise, it is necessary to seek appropriate accommodations of Aboriginal interests in light of the issues expressed in consultations.

Establishing legal norms for the purposes of reconciliation may be ne-cessary to promote efforts at reconciliation and to protect the rights of different parties. However, if establishing legal norms encourages parties on either side to seek to do the minimum permitted, it will not have the positive outcomes that real efforts at consultation and reconciliation could have. Some have raised the concern that governments may exploit the fact that the duty to consult does not include a veto by Aboriginal commun-ities to authorize developments after an attempt at consultation, imposing their views in the shorter term but with a risk of longer-term problems.[72] Consultation has much more potential than this scenario. Consultation embodies the possibility of genuinely hearing one another and seeking reconciliations that work in the shorter-term while opening the door for negotiations of longer-term solutions to unsolved legal problems. Those potentially engaged with consultations, whether governments, Aborig-inal communities, or corporate stakeholders, ought to bear in mind not only their doctrinal legal position but the longer-term prospects for good policy, for trust, and for reconciliation that will enable all to live together in the years ahead.

---

72 For one media discussion, see Konrad Yakabuski, "Hydro-Québec a Slow Learner on Native Rights," *Globe & Mail* (12 Mar. 2009) B2.

4

The Law in Action of the Duty to Consult

4.1 Introduction: The Concept of the Law in Action

It is customary in a legal text to write as if the basic legislation and case law on an issue sum up all there is to know on the law. Roscoe Pound famously resisted this approach, offering in 1910 a call for an analysis of not just the "law in books" but the "law in action."[1] Pound argued that the two would diverge, particularly in circumstances where social change rendered the settled law less relevant, where rigid legislation did not allow flexibility, and where administrative machinery was not fully functioning.[2]

The basic concept of the "law in action" is more inspired than the analysis Pound sets out, for there are other reasons why the "law in action" might differ from the "law in books," some of them originating from reasons opposite to the ones Pound cites. For example, there will be circumstances in which high-level appellate court pronouncements will provide insufficient detail for doctrine to work in applied contexts. Nonetheless, Pound's basic concept resonates in powerful ways, calling for attention beyond the law books to the law in action.

Pound's basic impulse to urge attention to the law in action does not strike readers today as shocking. Indeed, some hundred years later there is danger that "legal realism" may undermine the careful analysis of doctrine and legal reasoning that is vital to the legal academy in helping to maintain the rule of law. The duty to consult is one area in which one would end up with a rather limited view of the law without some attempt to come to grips

---

1 Roscoe Pound, "Law in Books and Law in Action: Historical Causes of Divergence Between the Nominal and Actual Law" (1910) 44 American Law Review 12.

2 *Ibid.* at 24.

with the law in action of the duty to consult. The duty to consult is being shaped not just in the courts but in the day-to-day policies and practices of governments, Aboriginal communities, and industry stakeholders. In the end, as will be argued later in this chapter, the coalescence of their efforts at implementing the law into action may well describe something vitally important about the law in this area.

4.2 Development of Governmental Consultation Policies

Within the structure of governments in Canada, constitutional rules obviously have supremacy over other documents, and legislation and regulations provide binding high-level guidance to government actors and those outside of government as well. Both legislation and regulations are created in more formal ways, legislation through the legislative assemblies and regulations through a particular mechanism of Cabinet approval and a notice period. Government policies are more malleable but are still an important means of guiding government actors as well as informing the public of how government actors will operate. It is often these policies, as well as simple day-to-day practice that have the most effect on how government actors will actually operate. The law in action will be more detailed and may even have a different flavour than the law in the books.

Provincial governmental policies related to the duty to consult have already been recognized as having significance for the doctrine. Note, for instance, the Supreme Court of Canada's reference in *Haida Nation* to the possible value of provincial policy:

> It should be observed that, since October 2002, British Columbia has had a Provincial Policy for Consultation with First Nations to direct the terms of provincial ministries' and agencies' operational guidelines. Such a policy, while falling short of a regulatory scheme, may guard against unstructured discretion and provide a guide for decision-makers.[3]

Upon the Supreme Court of Canada's move toward the modern, proactive duty to consult in *Haida Nation*, governments reacted swiftly with a first wave of duty to consult policies. The initial wave of policy

---

3   *Haida Nation* v. *British Columbia (Minister of Forests)*, [2004] 3 S.C.R. 511, 2004 SCC 73 at para. 51.

documents were often on an interim basis and geared toward using the mechanism of government policy documents to try to ensure that different government actors were complying with the legal requirements resulting from the new case law.[4] As a result, many of these policies were developed quickly and designed simply around the recently changed case law. They typically had not themselves followed upon consultation, and this gave rise in some instances to controversy. More recently, there has been a move toward a new set of consultation policies, often following on consultation, although the picture of how the main policies interact with other documents is not actually entirely straightforward and requires further description and analysis.

Saskatchewan's process over recent years helps to illustrate some of this development and also shows some of the challenges related to the stability of these policy frameworks. As in other jurisdictions, following the major developments in the Supreme Court of Canada in the Haida Nation trilogy, the government issued duty to consult guidelines to relevant stakeholders in June 2006. These guidelines, however, were based simply on legal doctrine as assessed by government lawyers without consultation with Aboriginal leaders, which led to criticism both from the Aboriginal community and the opposition Saskatchewan Party at the time.[5] Following the fall 2007 election, the new government launched a process on the duty to consult policy, releasing an interim policy in January 2008 before holding consultations with stakeholders that culminated in a Roundtable in Saskatoon in May 2008 attended by several hundred people.[6] This led to a

---

4   Examples included: Saskatchewan's Interim Guide for Consultation with First Nations and Métis People (Jan. 2008): www.fnmr.gov.sk.ca/documents/policy/consultguide.pdf; Manitoba, Provincial Policy for Consultation with Aboriginal Peoples (Jul. 2007): www.gov.mb.ca/ana/pdf/draft_aboriginal_consultation_policy_and_guidelines.pdf; Ontario, Draft Guidelines for Ministries on Consultation with Aboriginal Peoples Related to Aboriginal Rights and Treaty Rights (Jun. 2006): www.aboriginalaffairs.gov.on.ca/english/policy/draftconsultjune2006.pdf; Quebec, Interim Guide for Consulting the Aboriginal Communities (2006): www.autochtones.gouv.qc.ca/publications_documentation/publications/guide-interimaire_en.pdf.

5   See Hansard, Standing Committee on Intergovernmental Affairs and Infrastructure No. 42 (16 Apr. 2007) – 25th Legislature (Sask.) Vote 25.

6   *Seeking Common Ground: Roundtable Conference on First Nations and Métis Consultation and Accommodation: Conference Report* (Regina: Government of Saskatchewan Ministry of First Nations and Métis Relations, 2008): www.

draft document issued in December 2008,[7] which again drew criticism, but the government did eventually move toward a final document nonetheless.[8] Although this document, the June 2010 Saskatchewan Consultation Policy Framework, never did receive official support from the Federation of Saskatchewan Indian Nations (FSIN), it has effectively guided the practical operations of the duty to consult in Saskatchewan.

That said, as is also typical in other jurisdictions, there is not one sole document that is entirely determinative on government policy on consultation. Apart from general provincial government policy frameworks, different departments promulgate policy frameworks specific to their needs. This is the case, for example, in Saskatchewan, with the Ministry of the Environment, which is affected by the duty to consult on a daily basis. In June 2007, the Ministry adopted *Operational Procedures for Consultations with First Nations and Métis Communities*,[9] which remained in place for a period of time even in the context of shifting general policy.

Following the Saskatchewan government's adoption of the June 2010 Consultation Policy Framework, the Ministry of Environment did come into compliance with that document. However, the Ministry of Environment has also more recently continued to develop its own approaches that further guide and define the practical implementation of the duty to consult. In particular, the Ministry of Environment developed and released in November 2012 a *Proponent's Guide* to assist industry project proponents in understanding the duty to consult.[10] In the process, it more specifically defined the role of project proponents in ways not elaborated within the

---

fnmr.gov.sk.ca/roundtable-conference-report.

7   *Saskatchewan, First Nation and Métis Consultation Policy Framework: Draft* (Dec. 2008).

8   Government of Saskatchewan, *First Nation and Métis Consultation Policy Framework* (June 2010): http://www.gr.gov.sk.ca/Consultations/Consultation-Policy-Framework.

9   Saskatchewan, Ministry of the Environment, *Operational Procedures for Consultations with First Nations and Métis Communities* (2007).

10   Government of Saskatchewan, Ministry of Environment, *Proponent's Guide: Consultation with First Nations and Métis in Saskatchewan Environmental Impact Assessment: Guidelines for Engaging and Consulting with First Nations and Métis Communities in Relation to Environmental Assessment in Saskatchewan* (November 2012): http://www.environment.gov.sk.ca/EAProponent-ConsultationGuidelines.

Consultation Policy Framework, thus effectively establishing further law in action on the duty to consult.

What is perhaps even more interesting is that the Ministry of Environment's policy development process in relation to the *Proponent's Guide* now seems to have resonated further within government policy-making processes. The Government of Saskatchewan's Ministry of Government Relations held a set of engagement sessions in the fall of 2012 and received comments over the subsequent months, leading ultimately to the release in November 2013 of another proponent handbook intended to operate on a more widespread basis.[11] The shift is toward encouraging early engagement between industry and Aboriginal communities in a manner not necessarily contained as explicitly within the *Consultation Policy Framework*. This shift is very likely a good thing for all concerned. But the development of these policy documents simply shows the complex path that government policy-making can follow in this area.

One challenge that arises is in relation to the stability of consultation policies. Within our democratic system, a government's consultation policy can even be a matter for debate during elections, as it was in Saskatchewan, resulting in the consultation framework varying over time in ways that may be difficult to predict for those interested in long-term policy stability. That kind of long-term policy stability is particularly important in the context of different kinds of resource development. In the context of mining, the lifespan of a mine will often be measured in decades and even the development of the mine measured in many years. A changing policy framework during that time period could raise significant concerns on the economics of the project. Those working on policy in this area need to be highly attentive to a complex balance of considerations, including obviously respect for rights claims but also including appropriate respect for the variety of factors that go into responsible resource development.

By this point, a number of years after the development of the new case law on the duty to consult, each Canadian jurisdiction has adopted some form of Cabinet-approved government-wide policy or guidelines on the duty to consult. Some of these have continued in the style of interim consultation policies based on court decisions as to be applied in the particular jurisdiction. Such a format is true, for instance, of British Columbia's 2010

---

11   Government of Saskatchewan, Ministry of Government Relations, *Proponent Handbook: Voluntary Engagement with First Nations and Métis Communities to Inform Government's Duty to Consult Process* (November 2013).

update of its 2002 policy[12] or of Manitoba's 2009 interim policy.[13]

Similarly, the federal government has continued to operate with consultation guidelines that are in the nature of an interim policy based on legal developments more than a publicly developed consultation policy.[14] In such jurisdictions, there are often additional policy documents developed by parts of the government that also influence what the policy or guidelines actually mean in practice. At the federal level, there are different consultation policies in specific contexts, such as the separate consultation policy elaborated by Parks Canada.[15] Some federal administrative bodies or decision-making boards that consider the duty to consult routinely have also adopted policies in relation to how they will incorporate the consideration of Aboriginal concerns in general or the duty to consult in particular in their decision-making processes. As an important example, the National Energy Board has adopted such a document.[16]

At the federal level, there has also been an important decision to carry out consultation on a "whole-of-government" approach, with the introduction in 2008 of the Major Projects Management Office that serves as a coordinating mechanism on major project reviews. As presently structured, the practices in relation to this office actually have important implications for how consultation actually works at the federal level. In addition, there is ongoing thought on consultation and the more expansive forms it

12 Province of British Columbia, *Updated Procedures for Meeting Legal Obligations When Consulting First Nations* (7 May 2010).

13 Government of Manitoba, *Interim Provincial Policy for Crown Consultations with First Nations, Métis Communities and Other Aboriginal Communities* (4 May 2009): http://www.gov.mb.ca/ana/pdf/interim_aboriginal_consultation_policy_and_guidelines.pdf.

14 Aboriginal Affairs and Northern Development Canada, *Aboriginal Consultation and Accommodation: Updated Guidelines for Federal Officials to Fulfill the Duty to Consult* (March 2011): http://www.aadnc-aandc.gc.ca/DAM/DAM-INTER-HQ/STAGING/texte-text/intgui_1100100014665_eng.pdf.

15 Parks Canada, *A Handbook for Parks Canada Employees on Consulting and Accommodation with Aboriginal Peoples* (March 2011). The document tends to focus on consultation as policy rather than as a response to rights.

16 Canada, National Energy Board, *Consideration of Aboriginal Concerns in National Energy Board Decisions* (July 2008): https://docs.neb-one.gc.ca/ll-eng/llisapi.dll/fetch/2000/90463/522930/522832/Consideration_of_Aboriginal_Concerns_in_National_Energy_Board_Decisions_(A0T5X3).pdf?nodeid=524268&vernum=0.

may have to take in the context of some mega-projects. For example, in the context of consideration of the Northern Gateway Pipeline by the National Energy Board and ultimately by Cabinet, the government commissioned a special report on issues related to Aboriginal communities, and the Eyford Report that resulted engages in some meaningful discussion of ways to further consultation within the whole-of-government approach.[17] There are particular challenges in the context of transportation infrastructure, like pipelines, that crosses the traditional territories of many Aboriginal communities whose views on particular projects will sometimes differ. In the context of major projects, there obviously must be consultation, but there must also be clarity that consultation does not inherently require unanimous agreement.

In terms of different kinds of policies, some provinces have developed more formalized policies that are based on larger consultations and not simply on the interpretation of existing case law. In the process, some of these policies seek to achieve outcomes reaching beyond the simple application of what implications the case law has. Instead, they actively structure the consultation practices in their respective jurisdictions. Four policies stand out as being of this nature and with each of these four having unique characteristics: those of Saskatchewan,[18] New Brunswick,[19] Alberta,[20] and Newfoundland and Labrador.[21]

---

17   *Forging Partnerships, Building Relationships: Aboriginal Canadians and Energy Development,* Report to the Prime Minister by Douglas R. Eyford (29 November 2013).

18   Government of Saskatchewan, *First Nation and Métis Consultation Policy Framework* (June 2010): http://www.gr.gov.sk.ca/Consultations/Consultation-Policy-Framework.

19   Province of New Brunswick, Aboriginal Affairs Secretariat, *Government of New Brunswick Duty to Consult Policy* (November 2011): http://www2.gnb.ca/content/dam/gnb/Departments/aas-saa/pdf/en/DutytoConsultPolicy.pdf.

20   Government of Alberta, *Policy on Consultation with First Nations on Land and Natural Resource Management, 2013* (3 June 2013): http://www.aboriginal.alberta.ca/documents/GoAPolicy-FNConsultation-2013.pdf The policy was brought into force in August 2013. It is also accompanied by draft Corporate Guidelines: http://www.aboriginal.alberta.ca/documents/GoACorpGuidelines-FNConsultation-2013.pdf; and a draft Consultation Matrix: http://www.aboriginal.alberta.ca/documents/GoAMatrix-FNConsultation-2013.pdf.

21   Government of Newfoundland and Labrador, *Aboriginal Consultation Policy on Land and Resource Development Decisions* (April 2013): http://www.exec.

The full details of these policies are of course of interest to those operating within each of the jurisdictions in question. But even some broad schematic points concerning major differences between them are more generally noteworthy. First, the intended coverage of these policies differs significantly. While Saskatchewan's policy provides for consultation with Métis communities, Alberta's does not, and neither does New Brunswick's (which actually applies only to consultation with fifteen identified Mi'gmag First Nations and Wolastoqiyik First Nations listed in an appendix to the document). The Newfoundland and Labrador policy, facing a different context yet again, specifies that its policy framework will apply only outside the context of land claims agreements to which Newfoundland and Labrador is a party. For example, it specifies that the government regards its consultation duties to the Inuit of Labrador as being fully determined by the *Inuit Land Claims Agreement* and not by the provincial consultation policy.

Any such choices around coverage of a provincial consultation policy, of course, do not change the fundamental constitutional underpinnings of the doctrine. Alberta's choice to exclude Métis communities from its consultation policy, for example, does not mean that the province does not owe consultation obligations to Métis communities. Rather, it says simply that if there are Métis rights that give rise to consultation obligations in some Alberta settings, the consultation practices will not necessarily be determined by the main policy document but may take more *ad hoc* forms. So, the exclusion may reflect simply a desire for greater flexibility. However, those operating in a jurisdiction with a policy that is not comprehensive do need to be watchful for possible implications of the underlying constitutional doctrine that may go beyond what is in the policy document.

Some of the provincial consultation policies also extend the matters over which consultation is to occur. Saskatchewan's policy again serves as an interesting example in that it is actually framed as applying not only in the context of impacts on Aboriginal or treaty rights, where consultation is constitutionally required, but also in the context of impacts on "[t]raditional uses of lands and resources" that may or may not relate to a constitutional right,[22] something which Alberta's policy also provides for,[23] but

---

gov.nl.ca/exec/igas/publications/Aboriginal_consultation.pdf.

22   Saskatchewan, *Consultation Policy Framework, supra* note 8 at 5.

23   Government of Alberta, *Policy on Consultation with First Nations on Land*

which New Brunswick's does not, except in the context of an impact on an Aboriginal or treaty right.[24]

Saskatchewan's policy also accepts the application of the consultation policy not only to administrative decisions of government but more generally to "[c]reating a new or amended piece of legislation, regulation, policy or strategic plan that may have the effect of limiting or altering the use of Crown lands and renewable resources."[25] New Brunswick's policy does not extend to legislative action but does, for instance, extend to the "creation, amendment or implementation of regulations, policies or procedures."[26] Alberta's policy similarly potentially applies to regulatory development but has a number of significant exclusions.[27] Each of these jurisdictions has thus sought to craft something workable in light of local needs.

That same theme emerges around the role of industry project proponents. Saskatchewan's 2010 policy initially took a fairly limited view of the role of project proponents, although later policy documents, including the 2013 Proponent Guide have arguably begun to adjust this approach. Alberta's policy, however, is organized around a very significant role for project proponents, particularly in situations with a lesser impact. The policy provides very specifically for delegated consultation on lower-level impact projects. Such delegated consultation will be pursuant to further guidelines, including guidelines that establish timelines.

The Newfoundland and Labrador approach, still to be fleshed out in further documents, is quite different from that in many other jurisdictions. It actually envisions a much more significant delegation of consultation. It also establishes an expectation that project proponents would offer accommodation measures relatively routinely. It sets out an aim "to ensure that land and resource development decisions minimize or, where reasonably practicable, eliminate potentially adverse impacts on asserted rights."[28] But this responsibility weighs heavily on one particular party: "The pro-

---

and *Natural Resource Management, 2013, supra* note 20 at 1.

24   *Government of New Brunswick Duty to Consult Policy, supra* note 19 at 3.

25   *Ibid.*

26   *Ibid.* at 3.

27   Government of Alberta, *Policy on Consultation with First Nations on Land and Natural Resource Management, 2013, supra* note 20 at 3.

28   Government of Newfoundland and Labrador, *Aboriginal Consultation Policy on Land and Resource Development Decisions, supra* note 21 at 1.

ject proponent is expected to make reasonable efforts to mitigate or, where reasonably practicable, eliminate potentially adverse impacts on asserted rights," with specific reference being made to the idea of "benefits-related expectations."[29]

This latter policy has already been subject to critique for its significant shift in the balance affecting project proponents, and there have been suggestions it may impact on the interest of project proponents in pursuing development in Newfoundland and Labrador.[30] The prediction of such impacts depends, of course, on many different factors. An expectation of impact benefit agreements is not unknown in other jurisdictions and, indeed, is even required in Nunavut under the *Nunavut Land Claims Agreement*.[31] Whether such requirements have impacted on business involvement is not a simple matter to measure. However, these discussions do make clear the possibility of real impacts from different jurisdictions' consultation policies. Within our system of federalism, different jurisdictions have the opportunity to craft different policy approaches and different jurisdictions should and will experience different results from their different policy frameworks. The way in which the duty to consult is operationalized may differ among provincial governments on matters that are not defined within the case law, thus showing how these policies may have a significant role in defining the legal framework of consultation. Matters will, of course, be more complicated where a provincial policy on such an issue diverges from an Aboriginal community's expressed policy, a matter to which this chapter will return.

In some provinces, there have been moves toward embodying consultation relationships not only in policy and not only in other guidelines, but even in legislation. British Columbia, facing the widest scope of Aboriginal title claims, was at one stage particularly interested in this approach. In addition to a provincial policy on consultation, a number of different government or government-associated entities had developed more specific consultation policies. These included, among others, the British Colum-

---

29   *Ibid.* at 7.

30   Sam Adkins, Stephanie Axmann, & Thomas Isaac, "Unprecedented Aboriginal Consultation Policy Released by Government of Newfoundland and Labrador," McCarthy Tetrault Bulletin (1 May 2013): http://www.mccarthy.ca/article_detail.aspx?id=6254.

31   Section 26 of the Nunavut Land Claims Agreement makes an Inuit Impact and Benefit Agreement a requirement before a major development project.

bia Utilities Commission[32] and the Ministry of the Environment (in even such a specific context as pest management).[33] With administrative decision-making boards and tribunals entered into considering duty to consult issue,[34] the provincial government also began mooting a more general "New Relationship" with the province's Aboriginal peoples that included an intention to offer economic accommodation.[35] Associated with this, prior to 2009, the British Columbia government was considering the possibility of legislation that would codify a number of duty to consult issues, in the form of a Recognition and Reconciliation Act. Aboriginal communities raised some concerns with the potential legislation, and it did not proceed in the contemplated form.

Although other states, notably Australia, have legislated extensively on Aboriginal title and on associated rights analogous to consultation (further discussed in Chapter 5), they do so without a constitutionalized Aboriginal rights provision. In Canada, apart from the political challenges associated with the difficult balancing involved, to legislate on Aboriginal rights or title would be legally challenging. Any more comprehensive legislation on the duty to consult would, quite frankly, be most likely to be legislation designed somehow to adjust the process on consultation to advance efficiency goals or address some major obstacles coming from the duty to consult. The legislation would then be defended based on the *Sparrow* justification test. No government has yet moved in that direction, although

32 British Columbia, Utilities Commission, First Nations Consultation in Proceedings Before the British Columbia Utilities Commission (2007): www.bcuc.com/Documents/Proceedings/2007/DOC_17239_C12-22_First-Nations-Consultationreferencedoc.pdf.

33 British Columbia, Ministry of the Environment, Integrated Pest Management, Draft Guidelines for IPM Proponents Conducting Consultations with First Nations (2006): www.env.gov.bc.ca/epd/ipmp/first_nations_cons_guide/draft_guide.htm.

34 This was definitively required after *Carrier Sekani Tribal Council* v. *British Columbia (Utilities Commission)*, 2009 BCCA 67, which provides a survey of past treatment of the duty to consult by administrative boards and tribunals, some of which took up the task willingly but some of which had been reluctant to undertake it. The Supreme Court of Canada decision in the case reinforced the point.

35 The New Relationship document that commits to the development of new consultation frameworks: www.gov.bc.ca/arr/newrelationship/down/new_relationship.pdf.

anonymous sources have identified at least one Canadian government that has to some degree contemplated something like it.

It is significantly more likely that we will see the inclusion of some consultation-related provisions in particular legislation that properly has consultation-related connections. Ontario does not have the same Aboriginal title claims at issue as does British Columbia. But it has had some difficult history in respect of certain mining contexts, which has helped lead it toward new legislative requirements. The challenging issues have included a dispute involving Platinex, an exploration company, with the Kitchenukmaykoosib Inninuwug community back in the 2006-08 period, a dispute that led to various injunctions and controversies,[36] with the company taking the view that the government had failed to address its responsibilities. Ultimately, Platinex abandoned an $80-million lawsuit against the Ontario government, in exchange for a lesser negotiated payment, and decided to cut its losses. More recently, a major dispute erupted in the context of Solid Gold's attempts to carry out exploration activities in the traditional territory of the Wahgoshig First Nation. The government informally suggested to Solid Gold that it engage with the First Nation in its area of exploration activity. However, in developments with some analogies to what had happened in the Platinex dispute, the company, seeking to act on its legal rights, decided not to pursue such engagement and rested upon the duty to consult being on government. The First Nation involved ended up pursuing litigation that resulted in an injunction against further activity,[37] which interfered with Solid Gold's ability to complete its work within a deadline resulting from its flow-through shares financing. Because of the problems arising, the company has ended up pursuing litigation against the Ontario government, though it is still unclear where this will lead.

In the end, Ontario has put extensive consultation-related requirements into statutory form in the context of its mining legislation and legislation concerning development in northern Ontario. The Ontario mining provisions establish procedures for exploration plans and permits during early-stage exploration and clarify various requirements related to Aboriginal

---

36   These included [2006] 4 C.N.L.R. 152 (Ont. Sup. Ct. J.); [2007] 3 C.N.L.R. 181 (Ont. Sup. Ct. J.); [2007] 3 C.N.L.R. 221 (Ont. Sup. Ct. J.); and 2008 ONCA 533, dealing with contempt proceedings against members of the First Nation.

37   *Wahgoshig First Nation* v. *Ontario*, 2011 ONSC 7708, [2012] O.J. No. 22 (Sup. Ct.), leave to appeal to Divisional Court denied by a full written decision 2013 ONSC 632 (25 January 2013).

consultation as part of these plans.[38] First Nations' involvement in land use planning in northern Ontario is also more generally entrenched.[39] The development of these changes followed chronologically on the Platinex dispute, and their entry into force came about after the Solid Gold problems. Actual, on-the-ground problems have thus led toward new statutory requirements.

These types of provisions in at least some legislative contexts, perhaps especially those like mining, may become more commonplace. Quebec's new mining legislation has also ended up including Aboriginal consultation provisions.[40] Indeed, the decision in the *Ross River Dena Council* case — discussed at greater length in Chapter 2 — has led Yukon's government to be required to modify its mining legislation so as to create opportunities for consultation.

Obviously, if governments create legislation on the duty to consult, that is a new form of law on the books. But apart from that law on the books — which has tended to be a minor part of different governments' moves — the array of government policies under development or on the books is already vast. The tendency has been toward yet more detailed policies. Policies and practices of provincial governments or ministries have become one of the important ways in which the Supreme Court of Canada's general guidance is carried into action, in the process both interpreting and adjusting that guidance to the needs of particular contexts.

4.3 Aboriginal Communities' Consultation Policies

Apart from provincial and federal governments, however, Canadian Aboriginal communities have developed their own consultation policies in several different forms, some being at the national or provincial level and some enunciated by specific Aboriginal communities. National and provincial organizations have asserted governments' duties to consult with them at an institutional level. For example, at the national level, the Assembly of First Nations has asserted a government obligation to consult it

---

38   In the mining context generally, these changes came from Phase 2 of the *Mining Amendment Act, 2009,* S.O. 2009, c. 21 and associated regulations.

39   This is in the new *Far North Act, 2010,* S.O. 2010, c. 18.

40   Quebec's Bill 70, adopted in December 2013, implements such requirements. For a discussion of some features of the new legislation, see http://mccarthy.ca/article_detail.aspx?id=6567.

about legislation that might affect Aboriginal interests.[41]

Casual students of Aboriginal law often miss the complex interplay of interests at stake.[42] The duty to consult doctrine has reawakened tensions among different levels and organizations of Aboriginal representation. The *Labrador Métis Nation*[43] case marked, in some respects, an important victory for representatives of non-status and Métis communities, with the judges ready to recognize them as appropriate consultation partners. There was a possibility, then, that the Congress of Aboriginal Peoples (CAP), which claims to represent Métis and non-status Indians, could become an appropriate consultation partner. Apparently in response, the Assembly of First Nations (AFN) issued statements rejecting any government use of CAP for consultation purposes, illustrating some of the tension between organizations.[44] CAP's newsletter later reiterated its perspective that the *Labrador Métis Nation* case was ground-breaking for the establishment of a duty to consult with CAP and its affiliated organizations where they meet conditions similar to those which the Labrador Métis Nation had met.[45]

There have also been tensions among wider organizations and their constituents. In some provinces, for instance, there have been tensions between provincial organizations and individual First Nations concerning whom the government should consult. In Saskatchewan, the Federation of Saskatchewan Indian Nations (FSIN) began elaborating a duty to consult policy in 2005,[46] one element being that the government would consult dir-

41   See Assembly of First Nations, Special Chiefs Assembly, Res. No. 59/2005 (Dec. 2005): afn.ca/article.asp?id=2079. This was reasserted by then-National Chief Phil Fontaine before a Senate committee: Testimony on Bill C-292, Proceedings of Standing Senate Committee on Aboriginal Peoples, Issue 11 — Evidence — Apr. 16, 2008: www.parl.gc.ca/39/2/parlbus/commbus/senate/ Com-e/abor-e/11evbe. htm?Language=E&Parl=39&Ses=2&comm_id=1.

42   See, for example, Joe Sawchuk, *The Dynamics of Native Politics: The Alberta Métis Experience* (Saskatoon: Purich, 1998).

43   *Labrador Métis Nation* v. *Newfoundland and Labrador (Minister of Transportation and Works)*, 2006 FCA 393.

44   See, for example, Assembly of First Nations, Special Chiefs Assembly, Res. No. 42/2007, "Denunciation of the Congress of Aboriginal Peoples" (Dec. 2007): www.afn.ca/article.asp?id=4071.

45   "Newfoundland & Labrador v. Labrador Métis Nation: Ground-breaking case for CAP" (Spring 2009), The Forgotten People [Congress of Aboriginal Peoples Newsletter] at 10-11: www.abopeoples.org/media/people.pdf.

46   See Federation of Saskatchewan Indian Nations (FSIN), Lands & Resources,

ectly with the FSIN, implicitly in place of individual First Nations. Several First Nations' chiefs appeared at the Saskatchewan government's round-table in May 2008 to speak against this position, asserting the ongoing need for consultation with individual First Nations, and the FSIN at the meeting backed away somewhat from its earlier position.[47] The Saskatch-ewan government's current duty to consult policy makes clear that it will consult directly with individual First Nations' elected representatives un-less those First Nations have explicitly delegated their authority to another organization. As a matter of course, however, the FSIN will be notified of certain types of province-wide consultations. And the FSIN has often con-tinued to become involved in consultations, and has made applications on consultation issues in the context of administrative board hearings at which individual First Nations were already involved.[48]

In general, consultation with First Nations is notably further ahead than consultation with Métis communities, owing partly to the simpler identifi-cation of legally authorized representatives of First Nations. Status Indians under the *Indian Act* have prescribed forms of representation, developed within the legislative framework and band practice. Although consulting with Aboriginal leaders under the *Indian Act* has the danger of perpetuat-ing and extending power structures that do not necessarily correspond to traditional or desired forms of governance, the advantage for status Indi-ans is that they have easily identified representatives for consultation pur-poses. Non-status Indians and Métis have already faced much neglect from governments, and the structure of the duty to consult risks reinforcing this neglect because it is not clear with whom consultation is to occur. The duty to consult may inadvertently enhance the power of already relatively ad-vantaged Aboriginal groups over more disadvantaged ones.

This situation has led to provincial organizations representing Métis

---

"Duty to Consult and Accommodate": www.fsin.com/landsandresources/du-tytoconsult.html. The paper describes early discussions with the government in the immediate wake of the Haida Nation decision through to the adoption of resolutions by the FSIN and the adoption of an FSIN consultation policy: www.fsin.com/legislativeassembly/downloads/ConsultationPolicy.pdf.

47 *Seeking Common Ground: Roundtable Conference on First Nations and Métis Consultation and Accommodation: Conference Report, supra* note 6 at 5, 6, 18 and 19.

48 See *Re Enbridge Pipelines Inc.* (Feb. 2008) 2008 LNCNEB 2, OH-4-2007 at paras. 127-31 (N.E.B.).

communities mobilizing to ensure that they will be recognized as consultation partners and trying to set out some terms of consultation relationships. In some instances they will also make applications at administrative hearings where they are concerned that project proponents have not sought to consult with Métis communities.[49] The Métis Nation of Alberta started with workshops on consultation in April 2008,[50] and then moved toward developing a consultation policy.[51] The Métis Nation of Ontario similarly went through community consultations in the course of developing a consultation policy.[52] The Métis Nation of Saskatchewan held a Duty to Consult conference in March 2009, seeking to develop responses to the federal and provincial policies that were open for comment at the time.[53] At least one local president urged that there be ongoing development of duty to consult policies by Métis communities themselves.[54] In the meantime, the Métis Nation of Saskatchewan adopted an interim policy,[55] on which it has continued some work since and may update at some stage.

---

49   See, for example, *Re Enbridge Pipelines Inc.*, *ibid.* at paras. 132, 143. In this latter example, however, the Métis Nation of Saskatchewan had difficulty identifying potential impacts of the project, due to the absence of a Métis traditional land use survey.

50   See metisbarefacts.blogspot.com/2008/04/duty-to-consult-alberta.html, as well as www.metis.org/getdoc/48e97004-0ce3-4f3e-ab29-9df726595e7d/Metis-Rights — Consultation- MNA2008.aspx.

51   Métis Nation of Alberta, Consultation Policy Package (Jul. 2008): www.metis.org/getdoc/fbf6af78-76fd-44b2-80f1-f0018029ce45/MNA_Consultation_Policy_Package_Jul._2008.aspx.

52   Métis Nation of Ontario, Towards a Consultation Framework for Ontario Métis – 2007/08 Community Consultations: What We Heard Report (Jul. 2008): www.metisnation.org/consultations/framework_final_report.pdf. See also Métis Consultation and Accommodation: A Guide for Government & Industry on Engaging Métis in Ontario: www.metisnation.org/consultations/PDF/Duty_to_Consult_Guide.pdf, offering several prescriptions to government and industry on how to consult with Métis communities in Ontario.

53   Robert Lafontaine, "Saskatchewan Métis Concerned About Duty to Consult" (Apr. 2009) 12:4 Eagle Feather News 11.

54   *Ibid.*

55   Initially on an interim basis, the Métis Nation of Saskatchewan offered its Statement of Principles on Métis Consultation and Accommodation (May 2008): www.mns.ca/pdfs/Statement%20of%20Principles.pdf.

Although corporate and government stakeholders will tend to identify Métis locals as the relevant consultation partner, the complex nature of Métis societies raises the risk that consultation with Métis locals alone will miss many broader issues.[56] As a result, Métis organizations have attempted to move toward regional consultation protocols. Both the Métis Nation of Ontario and the Métis Nation of British Columbia's consultation guidelines moved in this direction.[57] Complex power dynamics and logistical questions are raised in the context of the duty to consult with different Aboriginal communities.

Aside from these broader developments, some individual Aboriginal communities also began to develop detailed consultation policies in an attempt to guide government and industry stakeholders who may need to consult with them. Many Aboriginal communities have given more specific indications on consultation issues apart from these detailed policies, with communities informing government representatives of certain consultation protocols in the course of consultation, but some communities have sought to develop more detailed policies in advance of consultation commencing.

One early policy was enunciated by the Northern Shuswap Tribal Council in 2003.[58] But some more detailed policies followed in the wake of the Supreme Court of Canada trilogy. In Alberta, the Horse Lake First Nation's Consultation Policy was an early example of an Aboriginal community setting out a relatively detailed policy concerning its expected modes of

---

56 For a summary of Métis governance structures, see Jason Madden, "The Métis Nation's Self- Government Agenda: Issues and Options for the Future," in Frederica Wilson & Melanie Mallet, *Métis-Crown Relations: Rights, Identity, Jurisdiction, and Governance* (Toronto: Irwin Law, 2008), p. 323. For historical background on the situation of the Métis in Canada, see Donald Purich, *The Métis* (Toronto: James Lorimer, 1988).

57 See Métis Nation of Ontario: www.metisnation.org/consultations; see also Métis Nation British Columbia, Consultation Guidelines (Feb. 2009): www.mpcbc.bc.ca/pdf/Final%20Consultation%20Guidelines.pdf.

58 Northern Secwepemc te Qelmucw (NStQ), Consultation and Accommodation Guidelines for Government and Third Parties, 1st edition (Jun. 2003). As of June 2009, the Northern Shuswap have released a new edition of their consultation guidelines: 2009 NStQ Consultation Guidelines: A Guide for Government and Third Parties (2009): www.nstq.org/Natural%20Resources/2009%20Northern%20Secwepemc%20te%20Qelmucw%20Consultation%20Guidelines.pdf.

consultation.[59] The Horse Lake First Nation (HLFN) Chief and Council authorized a representative to undertake and direct consultation processes out of the HLFN Industry Relations Corporation offices in Edmonton.[60] The HLFN Industry Relations Corporation, in turn, offered to provide consultation expertise to other First Nations, so this policy could potentially spread more broadly. It is premised on a model of direct negotiations with government decision-makers or lead individuals in industry, as opposed to governments and industry sending agents on their behalf. Unlike the situation of First Nations who depend on government funding, the Horse Lake model is operated on a fee-for-service basis. The policy sets out various parameters of the Horse Lake First Nation's interpretation of the existing law on consultation, including an expectation of economic accommodation in appropriate cases.

Other First Nations have also moved toward establishing duty to consult policies, although possibly not at the pace that some may have anticipated. Thunderchild First Nation near Turtleford, Saskatchewan, developed a Consultation Policy in July 2007, which it sent to the government and industry representatives, and established a Duty to Consult Office in August 2007.[61] However, only a handful of other Saskatchewan First Nations appear to have developed formal consultation policies in the years subsequent, and the picture is likely not different elsewhere. The development of a formal consultation policy involves a significant investment of resources, with a potentially uncertain return given that its effects may not be certain. Different communities will be positioned differently in terms of their capacity to develop such policies, and it is not surprising that a limited number of communities have undertaken the task.

Government and industry stakeholders have tended to be clear that they will not necessarily defer to the entirety of such policies but would, rather, follow parts of the Aboriginal communities' policies where they were not inconsistent with doctrinal law or their own policies, several suggesting that this would be for the sake of good relations with Aboriginal communities. Some provincial policies on consultation appear to suggest an even

---

59   Horse Lake First Nation Consultation Policy: www.horselakefirstnation.com/ consultation-policy.html.

60   *Ibid.*

61   Thunderchild First Nation, "Duty to Consult Report": www.thunderchild.ca/ default.aspx?ID=Duty%20to%20consult.

greater role for Aboriginal communities' policies where possible.[62] This degree of deference is not insignificant, but marks an accession to partial processes of Aboriginal law-making. In some instances, Aboriginal communities themselves consider the elaboration of these policies as important assertions of their rights and jurisdiction.

It still remains to be tested in the courts how these policies would interact with doctrinal requirements that Aboriginal communities be engaged in good faith consultations, but the possibility that the courts will give some meaningful weight to these policies and effectively co-jurisdiction over elements of consultation processes should not be disregarded. One existing example appears in the British Columbia Environmental Appeal Board's decision in *Xats'ull First Nation* v. *Gibraltar Mines Ltd.*,[63] in which the dissenting panel member referred to the government's failure to look at the consultation guidelines elaborated by the Xats'ull tribal council as one of the factors in her decision that the government had failed to carry out adequate consultation with the First Nation.[64] Governments obviously cannot be legally obligated to follow every measure in an Aboriginal community's consultation policy if, for instance, an Aboriginal community were to adopt a policy containing requirements not contained in the law itself. However, it would not be unreasonable to expect that governments have regard to elements of Aboriginal communities' consultation policies that are not inconsistent with the legal doctrine. To the extent that there are legal obligations to develop consultation systems collaboratively with those who are being consulted, governments might actually be obligated to do so. Aside from any legal obligation, there are other good reasons for government and industry stakeholders to consider seriously the approaches mandated in Aboriginal communities' consultation policies. Doing so would likely promote good will and longer-term positive outcomes. Aboriginal policies will sometimes have normative force outside of legal doctrine per se.

---

62   Ontario, Draft Guidelines for Ministries on Consultation with Aboriginal Peoples Related to Aboriginal Rights and Treaty Rights (Jun. 2006), *supra* note 4 at 16-17.

63   *Xats'ull First Nation* v. *Director, Environmental Management Act*, 2006-EMA-006(a), at para. 412: www.eab.gov.bc.ca/ema/2006ema006a.pdf.

64   *Ibid.* at paras. 369-376, 392, 411.

4.4 Development of Corporate Consultation Policies

As discussed in Chapter 2, duty to consult issues will often have major implications for corporate stakeholders as well as for governments and Aboriginal communities. This is particularly the case in the context of corporations involved in activities that need to be on certain lands, and where the sphere of their activity crosses Aboriginal traditional territories — a situation that will inevitably arise with companies involved in resource extraction and pipeline construction. As a result, it is not surprising that corporations have also developed consultation policies and, in some instances, put major efforts into them. Some industry stakeholders have developed full policies, and some larger resource companies have established multi-person units devoted to consultations. The scale of these operations should not be surprising; some corporations need to consult with dozens of Aboriginal communities in a given year. Just as one example, a securities filing by Talisman Energy in the early years of the duty to consult reported consultations with 11,500 people across five jurisdictions in relation to 1,358 projects in 2006 alone.[65]

As with governments and Aboriginal communities, the development of policies by corporations may also implicitly affect the normative framework within which the duty to consult operates. In some contexts involving the implementation of international law at national levels, corporate policies may fundamentally shape the way legal norms are applied and, indeed, involve corporations in what are, in essence, law-making processes. This phenomenon is described in the innovative work of UBC law professor Natasha Affolder, who notes that, in an international law context, "corporate engagement with treaty norms is a two-way street. Corporate behaviour can be altered by corporate interaction with these norms. But international norms can also be affected by their translation or capture by corporations."[66] Given the important role of corporate stakeholders in the duty to consult, the possibility that corporate policies and practices may be helping to shape the normative framework for the ongoing development of the duty should not be overlooked.

The development of corporate policy on the duty to consult is, of course,

---

65   Talisman Energy Corporate Responsibility Report 2006: www.sec.gov/Archives/edgar/data/201283/000110465907023381/a07-8413_1ex99d2.htm.

66   Natasha Affolder, "Is International Law an Effective Eco-Lobbying Tool?" (2008). Am. Soc. Int'l L. Proc. 63.

constrained by the size of the entities. In the context of mineral extraction, it may well be that junior exploration companies have few resources to invest in the development of duty to consult policies, whereas major mining companies may have greater resources to do so. These differentiations may have implications for the practicalities of the doctrine and may, for instance, dictate certain approaches to when the duty to consult is considered to be triggered, as discussed in Chapter 2.

That said, junior companies may be able to draw on industry norms and guidelines. In some instances, government departments involved in assisting industry may provide guidelines, as the Saskatchewan Mineral Exploration and Government Advisory Committee has done.[67] Government departments may provide other tools that may also be useful. For instance, Natural Resources Canada produced a Mining Information Kit for Aboriginal Communities designed to explain a proposed exploration program to potentially affected Aboriginal communities.[68] In other instances, the pooled efforts of industry may allow for the development of policy documents. The Mining Association of Canada developed a set of guiding principles on sustainable mining and Aboriginal communities.[69] Although geared to development companies, this document represents the first phase of an industry-wide effort to establish principles to guide mine development. The Saskatchewan Mining Association, similarly, has developed a Best Management Practice to serve as a practical guide on working relations with Aboriginal communities.[70]

Thus, even junior companies may be able to access legal resources without incurring the costs of developing policies on their own. That being said, the majors obviously have an advantage in the resources they can devote

---

67 Saskatchewan, Ministry of the Environment, Mineral Exploration Guidelines for Saskatchewan (Nov. 2007): www.environment.gov.sk.ca/adx/aspx/adxGetMedia.aspx?DocID=1512,803,531,94,88,Documents&MediaID=754&Filename=Mineral+Exploration+Guidelines.pdf.

68 Natural Resources Canada, Mining Information Kit for Aboriginal Communities (2006): www.nrcan.gc.ca/mms/pdf/mining_toolkit.pdf.

69 Mining Association of Canada, Towards Sustainable Mining Guiding Principles: Draft Framework for Mining and Aboriginal Peoples (Dec. 2006): www.mining.ca/www/media_lib/TSM_Documents/2006_Protocols/Draft_Aboriginal_Framework_Final.pdf.

70 Saskatchewan Mining Association, Best Management Practice 14 (May 2007): www.saskmining.ca/pdf/BMP14_1May07.pdf.

to consultation initiatives. Major companies may have developed duty to consult policies, but it would be naïve to assume that they will make these policies public. A well-developed consultation policy will, in some instances, be a competitive advantage. As an unexpected side effect of a legal doctrine, the competition among types of enterprises may have shifted in complex ways.

Indeed, the role of the duty to consult doctrine may reshape the business landscape in favour of corporations that are able to enter into effective relationships with Aboriginal communities. Interestingly, there have been limited moves by Asian nations to enter into "nation-to-nation" discussions with Canadian Aboriginal communities with the aim of gaining access to natural resources on Aboriginal lands; Chinese and Korean investors began at one stage to put hundreds of millions of dollars into a hedge fund that will pursue related opportunities.[71] Just what these developments might mean in future remains to be seen.

In some instances, of course, corporate practices may be as important or more important than formalized corporate policies. Some practices will end up identifying potentially affected Aboriginal communities based on a so-called "consultation corridor" which would include Aboriginal communities within a particular distance of a pipeline right of way.[72] Following on the identification of potentially affected communities, the corporation may seek to consult only with those communities within the corridor, making it less likely that other Aboriginal communities will become involved.

In other instances, corporate practice is instantiating corporate policy in particular ways geared to negotiation with Aboriginal communities. Enbridge Inc., a major Canadian pipeline company, has featured in media reports alluding to the practice. Enbridge, which is engaged in oil pipeline expansion projects that cross traditional Dakota lands in Saskatchewan and Manitoba, negotiated a memorandum of understanding with five Dakota First Nations in Manitoba in 2007, with an extension in late 2008 lead-

---

71   Joe Friesen, "Asian Investors Back Natives Bands: Hedge Fund Focused on Developing Aboriginal Land Popular in China, Korea," *Globe & Mail* (9 Mar. 2009) A5.

72   See *Re Enbridge Pipelines Inc.*, *supra* note 48 at paras. 119-24, detailing the identification of potentially affected groups through the use of a 160 km consultation corridor. See also *Re TransCanada Keystone Pipeline GP Ltd.* (Sept. 2007), 2007 LNCNEB 9, OH-1-2007 at para. 127 (N.E.B.), detailing the identification of potentially affected groups within a 50 km corridor.

ing to the payment of $100,000 to each of these First Nations.[73] Although these First Nations had originally sought intervenor status at the National Energy Board hearings, they withdrew their application on signing the memorandum of understanding.[74] Enbridge also engaged in negotiation in the context of protests slowing traffic near its pipeline compound east of Regina.[75] After a week of protests, chiefs from Treaty 4 and Treaty 6 First Nations participated in a pipe ceremony with Enbridge officials to mark a confidential deal under which Enbridge apparently agreed to provide increased skills training, jobs, and contracts, as well as living allowances to some individuals in training.[76] A spokesperson for the Treaty 4 chiefs spoke of hope for the future, saying, "We're looking at equity in future projects on this pipeline and other energy projects that Enbridge has and looking at some of their assets. We're looking at long-term revenue streams, looking at securing some of those for Treaty 6 and Treaty 4 territorial communities."[77] Corporate practices of this sort combined with Aboriginal communities' expectations may well have implications for others in that they develop practices in relation to economic accommodation or compensation.

These particular developments are just one small instance of a much larger pattern of negotiation between industry stakeholders and Aboriginal communities, fostered in large part by the duty to consult. Many such arrangements are not widely publicized. However, as in the discussion in earlier chapters on impact benefit agreements, one can note the significant development of negotiated arrangements between industry stakeholders and Aboriginal communities.

For a number of years now, Canadian companies have begun including references on the implications of the duty to consult in their documenta-

---

73 Matt Goerzen, "Pipeline firm strikes deal with Man. First Nations," *Saskatoon StarPhoenix* (13 Jan. 2009), A5.

74 *Ibid.* The National Energy Board decision on Enbridge's application noted these First Nations' support for the project following Enbridge's Aboriginal engagement efforts: *Re Enbridge, supra* note 48 at para. 124.

75 See Joe Friesen, "Dispute Shuts Alberta Clipper Pipeline," *Globe & Mail* (1 Oct. 2008) A6; Barb Pacholik, "Company, First Nations hold meeting," *Saskatoon StarPhoenix* (30 Sept. 2008) A11.

76 James Wood & Lana Haight, "Pipeline company, First Nations reach 'new alliance,'" *Saskatoon StarPhoenix* (4 Oct. 2008), A3.

77 *Ibid.*

tion to shareholders.[78] In Australia, which has a longer experience with more specific statutory norms in relation to Native title and procedural rights paralleling the duty to consult, companies have gone on to significant analysis and practice in relation to the financial, accounting, and auditing implications that arise in connection with potential Native title claims.[79] Canadian firms have yet to face these issues fully. Although some securities filings have referenced duty to consult issues,[80] there have been issues regarding possible inadequate reporting on them, leading in some instances to investor unrest. For example, as early as the May 2009 annual meeting of Enbridge Inc., one investing fund sought clarification on the risks of non-approval of the Northern Gateway Pipeline posed by the duty to consult.[81]

Many business dimensions of the duty to consult require urgent attention, but as attention is directed to these various dimensions, corporate policy and practice, which develops implicitly, says something about the expected shape of the duty to consult, shaping its form within the "law in action." Corporate policies and practices, however, continue to develop under the influence of the duty to consult doctrine. Corporate stakeholders' policies are playing a major role in the developing "law in action" of the duty to consult, entering into engagements of conflict or coalescence with government and Aboriginal policies and practices.

---

78 For some earlier examples from SEC filings, see filings by Starfield Resources Inc.: www.sec.gov/Archives/edgar/data/1074795/000095013308002953/w65774e20vf.htm at p. 6; Oilsands Quest Inc.: www.sec.gov/Archives/edgar/data/1096791/000103570408000299/d58004e10vk.htm at p. 29; Cameco: www.sec.gov/Archives/edgar/data/1009001/000113031908000282/o39572exv99w1.htm; Fording Canadian Coal Trust: www.sec.gov/Archives/edgar/data/1158113/000136231008001452/c72727exv99wa.htm at p. 34.

79 See Craig Jackson & Michael Bray, "Financial, Accounting and Auditing Implications," in Bryan Horrigan & Simon Young (Eds.), *Commercial Implications of Native Title* (Sydney: Federation Press, 1997), p. 200; and Bryan Horrigan, "Practical Implications for Financiers, Land Dealers, Investors and Professional Advisers," in *ibid.* p. 215.

80 See *supra* note 78.

81 See David Ebner, "Investor Urges Enbridge to Assess Risk of Delay," *Globe & Mail* (30 Mar. 2009) B1.

4.5 Policies, Practices, and the Formation of "Law"

The specific interactions of government policies, Aboriginal communities' policies, and industry stakeholder policies open points at which there may be coalescence among the different policies. At these points of coalescence, all stakeholders may end up acting harmoniously. At points where the policies of different stakeholders diverge, there may be power-based struggles between different stakeholders, with different positions emerging at different points in time. In the absence of direct intervention by the courts, the interactions of policy may yield something amounting to "law."

However, other situations can also arise. Where a province delegates some project-specific activities to industry project proponents, its perspectives on how consultation is to occur may clash with those of some First Nations. Some First Nations' consultation policies have indicated that they will not accept consultation with anyone other than government or the lead proponents. In an instance where a province attempts to delegate consultation to industry stakeholders who then attempt to consult with a First Nation that refuses to consult with them, matters will be put to the test. Each party will have to think about the possible reactions of the courts. If the First Nation refuses to consult with industry stakeholders, the courts might conclude that the government has fulfilled its duty to consult — or the courts might consider that the government has failed in that duty. It is quite possible that the parties will come to some solution in these circumstances, perhaps with government choosing not to delegate consultation in the particular situation or perhaps with the First Nation agreeing to carry out limited consultation with industry representatives. A practice that finds some way through the interstices of the different policy frameworks will create the means by which the duty to consult is carried out, thus defining the legal duty to consult through the practice of interacting stakeholders.

The particular practices that arise from initial disagreements may or may not endure, depending on whether the parties involved are willing to adapt their view to what the legal context of the duty to consult requires of them. In instances where different stakeholders are in agreement on certain practices and these are legally required — whether from the outset or through some adaptation of views — it is worth noting that the practices resulting would potentially meet requirements analogous to those required for the formation of customary international law, or perhaps customary law more generally. Consistent practice accompanied by a belief that it is legally required arguably creates a sort of customary norm, admittedly subject to alteration through other legal sources, but one that nonetheless creates a normative framework. Thus, there arises the interesting possibility that points of coalescence between these frameworks generate a sort of customary normative order.

It is not the purpose of this book to enumerate a new source of law, but it is worth noting the possible development of specific forms of normative order in the context of the overarching duty, with governments, Aboriginal communities, and industry stakeholders coalescing around different needs in different parts of Canada to develop workable means of specifying the duty to consult in localized forms.

As this phenomenon develops, there may be specific reference to the policies of different organizations. Already we see that corporate policies can interact with government decision-making processes, as administrative boards will sometimes refer to corporate policies in enumerating their expectations of particular corporations.[82] We have not yet seen the citing of Aboriginal communities' policy frameworks, but, as noted earlier, these policies could in some instances have an impact. There may develop an interplay among the policy documents of governments, Aboriginal communities, and industry stakeholders.

David Szablowski has examined a related phenomenon in the context of interactions between Indigenous communities in developing countries, mining companies, and the World Bank.[83] He argues that the overlapping of different legal orders in a phenomenon that he calls "interlegality"[84] can lead to the constitution of a new legal order at the intersections of these legal orders and interpretations of them. The possibility that norms created in one order can create a bargaining endowment — in simpler terms, an advantage in negotiation processes — allows for a migration of norms

---

82   For some early examples, see *Re Enbridge Pipelines Inc., supra* note 48 at paras. 119ff., discussing Enbridge's Indigenous Peoples Policy; *Re TransCanada Keystone Pipeline GP Ltd., supra* note 72 at paras. 127ff., referring to TransCanada's Aboriginal Relations Policy; and *Re SemCAMS Redwillow ULC* (Mar. 2009), 2009 LNCNEB 3, No. GH-2-2008 at paras. 91ff. (N.E.B.), discussing the SemCAMS Aboriginal Engagement Guidelines and Consultation Protocols.

83   David Szablowski, *Law and Local Struggles: Mining, Communities, and the World Bank* (Oxford: Hart, 2007).

84   *Ibid.* at 292.

among different orders and ultimately a legal terrain that forms from the combination of different perspectives on the relevant legal orders.[85]

4.6 Conclusion

If this chapter has in some ways seemed to be offering a long list of different policy frameworks, that has been part of its goal. The diversity of sources commenting on the duty to consult is itself significant, and illustrates the role that many people and institutions in society, beyond the courts, have in the development of the doctrine.

Roscoe Pound argues that "[i]t is the work of lawyers to make the law in action conform to the law in the books, not by futile thunderings against popular lawlessness, nor eloquent exhortations to obedience of the written law, but by making the law in the books such that the law in action can conform to it."[86] The development of different legal approaches to the duty to consult within the policies and practices of government, Aboriginal, and industry stakeholders speaks to something that is missing in the elaboration of the duty to consult doctrine by the courts. In this instance, though, it may be proper for the courts to hold back. Just as the Supreme Court of Canada is allowing the lower courts to develop elements of the doctrine in accordance with traditional common law, so, too, the courts can generally allow stakeholders to develop practices that can illuminate what is valuable in and what is challenging about the law in this area. This approach is obviously decentralizing to courts in this area, but some of the theoretical approaches to the duty to consult discussed in Chapter 1 point to how the courts see the duty to consult doctrine as a means of the courts themselves not overstepping their functional roles.

The possibility of diverse approaches within a diverse country, developed by means other than through the courts, offers the possibility of a level of detail in the doctrine that the courts simply cannot achieve in the same way. A rich body of policy and practice is emerging that can respect jurisdictional specificities, the needs of different Aboriginal communities, the economics of different industry stakeholders, and ultimately the interests of all involved. The law in action of the duty to consult is an important element of understanding the doctrine.

---

85   *Ibid.* at 289-305.

86   Pound, *supra note 1* at 36.

5

International Law and the Duty to Consult

5.1 Introduction

The duty to consult obviously contains the seeds of its own future growth, and the examination of the case law in Chapters 2 and 3 has already suggested some directions in which the courts are developing the doctrine. Chapter 4 has shown how significant developments in the doctrine are also taking place outside the legal system, in the strict sense, and are being effected through the development of government policy documents, Aboriginal communities' own duty to consult policies, and corporate policies and practices related to the duty to consult. These chapters have suggested some ways in which the doctrine is evolving in response to the needs it serves.

Those needs, however, represent only some of the contexts relevant to the ongoing development of the doctrine. One other important source of future development for the duty to consult is in international law. The Canadian approach to the duty to consult is situated within the context of a larger set of international law norms on the rights of Indigenous peoples, and these norms have important interactions with the Canadian duty to consult doctrine.

To the extent that the duty to consult doctrine fulfills the obligations of international law in respect of Canada's treatment of Indigenous communities,[1] evolving international law standards may imply future

---

1   For seminal international law writings on the rights of Indigenous peoples, see S. James Anaya, *Indigenous Peoples in International Law,* 2nd Edition (Oxford: Oxford University Press, 2004); Russell Lawrence Barsh, "Indigenous Peoples: An Emerging Object of International Law" (1986) 80, Am. J. Int'l L. 369; Siegfried Wiessner, "Rights and Status of Indigenous Peoples: A Global Comparative and International Legal Analysis" (1999) 12 Harv. Hum. Rts. J.

developments of the duty to consult. To the extent that other domestic systems of consultation have grown in states that may influence Canada, these approaches are worthy of consideration for what they may imply for Canada's duty to consult doctrine in future because of both their possible direct relevance and their influence through the international law system. This Chapter seeks to examine this important possible influences on the future shape of the duty to consult doctrine.

Chapter 6 will return to some of the theoretical perspectives on the duty to consult set out in Chapter 1 to consider them alongside the more elaborated content of the doctrine as discussed throughout the book. It will be possible to assess whether the more elaborated doctrine has implications for how those theories describe it — or their degree of "fit" with the doctrine.[2] Only with this compilation of doctrine from the lower courts, the policies and practices of various stakeholders, and the possible international and comparative influences, will it be possible to come to a fuller understanding of the duty to consult.

5.2 Key International Law Concepts

To understand the implications of international law on Indigenous issues in general or of particular instruments like the *United Nations Declaration on the Rights of Indigenous Peoples*, it is helpful to ground the discussion in a clear understanding of the nature of international law and of its impacts on domestic legal systems. International law — traditionally, that body of law governing the conduct of states, or at least developing at the international level — develops in a manner very different than law within the domestic legal systems with which most readers will be familiar.

There is no authoritative international legislative body or court system

---

57; Benedict Kingsbury, "Reconciling Five Competing Conceptual Structures of Indigenous Peoples' Claims in International and Comparative Law" (2001) 34 N.Y.U.J. Int'l L. & Pol. 189; and Alexandra Xanthaki, *Indigenous Rights and United Nations Standards: Self-Determination, Culture, and Land* (Cambridge: Cambridge University Press, 2007). Mauro Barelli is also currently finishing an important new book on Indigenous rights and the international law system.

2   Early in Chapter 1, the roles of "fit" and "soundness" were discussed as important elements in testing the application of different theoretical approaches, following Ronald Dworkin's *Law's Empire* (Cambridge: Belknap, 1986).

as there are in domestic legal systems. International law develops, rather, through the consent of states, predominantly through two major sources: states may subscribe to international legal obligations through signing and ratifying treaties (also called "conventions") with other states; and what is called "customary international law" can develop where there is uniform state practice and evidence of *opinio juris* —the requirement that this practice arises in a context where states believe themselves to be legally bound to act as they do. I will return at the end of this chapter to make a claim about developing customary international law on consultation, but that statement will be possible based only on the discussion of the full chapter.

In the meantime, in the context of Indigenous rights, one major convention or treaty that has been adopted by some states is ILO Convention No. 169 of 1989.[3] This Convention has been ratified by a limited number of states, principally in Latin America and in Europe, and it creates binding legal obligations only for those states that have ratified it. However, it set forth two consultation-related obligations that have helped shape subsequent discussions. The ILO Convention commits in Article 6:

> 1. In applying the provisions of this Convention, Governments shall:
> (a) Consult the peoples concerned, through appropriate procedures and in particular through their representative institutions, whenever consideration is being given to legislative or administrative measures which may affect them directly;
> (b) Establish means by which these peoples can freely participate, to at least the same extent as other sectors of the population, at all levels of decision-making in elective institutions and administrative and other bodies responsible for policies and programmes which concern them;
> (c) Establish means for the full development of these peoples' own institutions and initiatives, and in appropriate cases provide the resources necessary for this purpose.
> 2. The consultations carried out in application of this Convention shall be undertaken, in good faith and in a form appropriate to the circumstances, with the objective of achieving agreement or consent to the proposed measures.[4]

---

3   International Labour Organization (ILO) Convention Concerning Indigenous and Tribal Peoples in Independent Countries (ILO No. 169) (1989), 72 ILO Official Bull. 59, entered into force Sept. 5, 1991.

4   *Ibid.*

A second, more specific duty arises in relation to resources, as set out in Article 15(2) of the ILO Convention:

> In cases in which the State retains the ownership of mineral or sub-surface resources or rights to other resources pertaining to lands, governments shall establish or maintain procedures through which they shall consult these peoples, with a view to ascertaining whether and to what degree their interests would be prejudiced, before undertaking or permitting any programmes for the exploration or exploitation of such resources pertaining to their lands. The peoples concerned shall wherever possible participate in the benefits of such activities, and shall receive fair compensation for any damages which they may sustain as a result of such activities.[5]

These provisions, as stated, bind only those states that have ratified ILO Convention No. 169. But they have helped shape discussion in the context of other evolving norms.

The sources of international law are enumerated in article 38(1) of the *Statute of the International Court of Justice,* with that article commonly being taken as a reasonably authoritative statement of the sources of international law. In addition to conventions and custom, it is also worth noting the existence of another source listed in article 38(1)(c), this being "general principles" of international law. The usual account of general principles of international law is that they are principles common across the different legal systems of the world, but there are other accounts of how such principles are identified about which I have written at greater length elsewhere.[6]

The concept of general principles is important in the present context especially because of a 2012 decision of the Inter-American Court of Human Rights in the *Sarayaku* v. *Ecuador* case. In this case concerning consultation with Indigenous communities, which could have been decided based on the ILO Convention 169 because Ecuador had ratified this treaty, the Court also chose to pronounce on a more general obligation. At the end of a paragraph filled with extensive citation to different national legal provisions — a mix of constitutional provisions, legislative provisions,

---

5   *Ibid.*

6   See, in particular, Michelle Biddulph & Dwight Newman, "A Contextualized Account of General Principles of International Law" (2014) 26 Pace International Law Review (forthcoming).

and judicial decisions — the Inter-American Court ends up stating that "[i]n other words, the obligation to consult, in addition to being a treaty-based provision, is also a general principle of international law."[7]

One international judicial decision does not necessarily bind other international courts and tribunals, and it thus does not necessarily definitively set out the state of international law. However, the Inter-American Court's conclusion that an obligation to consult Indigenous peoples is a "general principle" (in the technical sense) of international law is significant. It is a statement from a respected international decision-making body that states must respect an obligation to consult Indigenous peoples concerning state activities that may affect them. To the extent such a requirement becomes part of international law, states are subject to an international requirement that they respect it. Were Canadian constitutional law to cease to provide for the duty to consult, and if Canadian governments then chose not to follow such an obligation, Canada could come into a position of being in breach of international law.

The effect of international law on Canadian domestic law, though, is actually complex. On the accepted position in Canada (which is different in some countries), treaties do not change Canadian domestic law unless legislators implement them through statutes. Customary international law theoretically becomes part of Canadian common law, unless Canadian legislators specifically choose otherwise. But it is highly unusual for parties to attempt to make arguments based on customary international law, partly because of the difficulties of proving its contents and partly because Canadian courts are simply not used to those arguments.

The effects of general principles of international law within domestic law are less commonly discussed. This is partly because the more widespread use of general principles is something of a recent phenomenon.[8] It is also possibly because it is tougher to explain what should happen with general principles directly derived from other legal systems. Any statement that Canadian law incorporates general principles of international law would amount, on the dominant account of general principles of international law, to a statement that Canadian law draws directly from widespread principles present in other legal systems. That is probably not the case. Canada

---

7   *Case of the Kichwa Indigenous People of Sarayaku* v. *Ecuador*, Judgement, Inter-AM. Ct. H.R. (Ser. C) No. 242, (June 27, 2012), at para. 164.

8   See Biddulph & Newman, *supra* note 6, for some of the history of general principles.

does regard other legal systems' principles often as persuasive, but that is different than saying that they automatically become part of Canadian law. Rather, Canada may be bound by and accountable to general principles at an international level. But it remains responsible to develop implementation of these principles domestically without them automatically becoming part of Canadian law. The recent statement from the Inter-American Court has some significance, but that significance is limited.

5.3 Implications of the *Declaration on the Rights of Indigenous Peoples*

More well-known, of course, than the statement of the Inter-American Court on consultation with Indigenous peoples as a general principle of international law is the developing argument that consultation is a norm of customary international law and that this is evidenced through the *United Nations Declaration on the Rights of Indigenous Peoples*.[9] That *Declaration* represented the culmination of decades of negotiation amongst states and representatives of Indigenous peoples, with Indigenous peoples thus entering to some degree into the international law-making process.[10] In many ways, then, it represents an instrument reflecting a major statement on the rights of Indigenous peoples. And, it includes major articles on consultation. The *Declaration* includes such provisions as Articles 18, 19, and 32:

> 18. Indigenous peoples have the right to participate in decision-making in matters which would affect their rights, through representatives chosen by themselves in accordance with their own procedures, as well as to maintain and develop their own indigenous decision making institutions.

---

9   *United Nations Declaration on the Rights of Indigenous Peoples*, U.N.G.A. Res. 61/295, U.N. Doc. A/RES/61/295 (13 Sept. 2007), (2007) 46 I.L.M. 1013.

10   For discussion of the negotiations, see James (Sa'ke'j) Youngblood Henderson, *Indigenous Diplomacy and the Rights of Peoples: Achieving UN Recognition* (Saskatoon: Purich, 2008). For discussion of the significance of Indigenous peoples being part of the law-making process and a justification of this inclusion, see Dwight Newman, "Norms of Consultation with Indigenous Peoples: Decentralization of International Law Formation or Reinforcement of States' Role," in Andrew Byrnes, Mika Hayashi, & Christopher Michaelsen (Eds.), *International Law in the New Age of Globalization* (Leiden: Brill, 2013).

19. States shall consult and co-operate in good faith with the indigenous peoples concerned through their own representative institutions in order to obtain their free, prior and informed consent before adopting and implementing legislative or administrative measures that may affect them.

32. (1) Indigenous peoples have the right to determine and develop priorities and strategies for the development or use of their lands or territories and other resources.

(2) States shall consult and co-operate in good faith with the indigenous peoples concerned through their own representative institutions in order to obtain their free and informed consent prior to the approval of any project affecting their lands or territories and other resources, particularly in connection with the development, utilization or exploitation of mineral, water or other resources.

(3) States shall provide effective mechanisms for just and fair redress for any such activities, and appropriate measures shall be taken to mitigate adverse environmental, economic, social, cultural or spiritual impact.[11]

These and other articles that refer to consultation also have text that refers to a concept of "free, prior, and informed consent." However, one must read the text carefully, and it has been subjected to important interpretations, notably a reading by the United Nations Special Rapporteur on the Situation of Human Rights and Fundamental Freedoms of Indigenous People in his 2009 Annual Report, which was focused on the duty to consult.[12] That Report suggests two important things. First, the language in a number of articles of the *Declaration* concerned with "free, prior, and informed consent" does not create a veto power, in that it does not create an obligation to have actually obtained consent but creates, rather, an obligation to engage in a good faith process with the genuine objective of obtaining consent, but which might fail to be obtained in some situations. Second, the phrasing of different articles is different, which shows an intention to create a spectrum of obligations, depending on the seriousness of impact on the Indigenous

---

11   *Declaration on the Rights of Indigenous Peoples, supra* note 9.

12   Annual Report of the United Nations Special Rapporteur on the Rights and Fundamental Freedoms of Indigenous People, U.N. Doc. A/HRC/12/34 (15 July 2009).

community affected by particular actions. I have argued elsewhere that the version of the *Declaration* offered by the Special Rapporteur in this report actually has a strong resemblance to the Canadian duty to consult doctrine, perhaps showing both some Canadian influence and some attempt to draw Canada onside with the *Declaration* at a time when Canada had not yet endorsed it[13]—with Canada's later endorsement of the *Declaration* being a subject of discussion momentarily.

Formally, the *Declaration* was adopted as a Resolution of the United Nations General Assembly. The dominant view in international law is that a resolution or declaration by the United Nations General Assembly does not inherently have any legal force.[14] In some instances, such resolutions will provide the basis for a future treaty or convention, but the legal force then attaches to the treaty or convention. In other instances, a General Assembly declaration or resolution may describe the state of customary international law, though it provides no independent force to change it. On some accounts, the votes for a General Assembly declaration or resolution, however, may themselves be discussed as acts of states that help establish state practice or *opinio juris,* and thus further the development of customary international law.[15]

The adoption of the *Declaration,* though, was not accomplished without controversy; indeed, it took some fourteen years of negotiation from the draft text and came close to facing a very sharply divided vote in the General Assembly, with many African states threatening to vote against the *Declaration* until a number of changes were secured.[16] In the end, the *Declaration* passed the General Assembly by a vote of 143 votes to 4, but with

---

13 See discussion in Newman, "Norms of Consultation with Indigenous Peoples," *supra* note 10.

14 For a number of discussions of this issue in the specific context of the *Declaration,* see the superb collection by Stephen Allen & Alexandra Xanthaki (Eds.), *Reflections on the UN Declaration on the Rights of Indigenous Peoples* (Oxford: Hart, 2011).

15 *Ibid.*

16 For discussion of the complex dynamics of the last-minute efforts to bring African states onside, see: Dwight Newman, "The Law and Politics of Indigenous Rights in the Postcolonial African State" (2008) 102 Am. Soc. Int'l L. Proceedings 69; Dwight Newman, "Africa and the United Nations Declaration on the Rights of Indigenous Peoples," in Solomon Dersso (Ed.), *Perspectives on the Rights of Minorities and Indigenous Peoples in Africa* (Pretoria: Pretoria University Law Press, 2010).

11 abstentions and 36 absences.[17] Many of the abstentions and absences were African states that likely had ongoing concerns with the *Declaration*.[18] The four votes against were states of particular significance within the Anglo-American legal world: Australia, New Zealand, the United States, and Canada.[19] Moreover, many states made interpretive declarations at the time of voting for the *Declaration* so as to indicate limits on what they were accepting.

All four states that voted against the *Declaration* have subsequently indicated their endorsement of it (this endorsement, notably, not being a "ratification" as with a treaty, despite constant media errors otherwise). However, this endorsement was probably eased by the cautious interpretations of it offered by the Special Rapporteur,[20] and each endorsement was also accompanied by an interpretive declaration intended to limit the legal effects of the endorsement. As just one example, Canada's endorsement was specific as to the view that the *Declaration* does not have legal force, with the endorsement stating in part as follows:

> The Declaration is an aspirational document which speaks to the individual and collective rights of Indigenous peoples, taking into account their specific cultural, social and economic circumstances. Although the Declaration is a non-legally binding document that does not reflect customary international law nor change Canadian laws, our endorsement gives us the opportunity to reiterate our commitment to continue working in partnership with Aboriginal peoples in creating a better Canada.[21]

---

17   UN Media Release, "General Assembly Adopts Declaration on Rights of Indigenous Peoples; 'Major Step Forward' Towards Human Rights For All, Says President," U.N. Doc GA/10612 (13 Sept. 2007): www.un.org/News/Press/docs/2007/ga10612.doc.htm.

18   See Newman, "The Law and Politics of Indigenous Rights in the Postcolonial African State," *supra* note 16.

19   UN Media Release, *supra* note 17.

20   See Newman, "Norms of Consultation with Indigenous Peoples," *supra* note 10.

21   Aboriginal Affairs and Northern Development Canada, "Canada's Statement of Support on the United Nations Declaration on the Rights of Indigenous Peoples" (12 November 2012): http://www.aadnc-aandc.gc.ca/eng/13093742 39861/1309374546142.

It also stated that "[w]e are now confident that Canada can interpret the principles expressed in the Declaration in a manner that is consistent with our Constitution and legal framework."[22]

Whatever the status of General Assembly resolutions generally, the honest if sad reality is that the *Declaration's* passage probably did not change international law as much as some might think. There is a need for caution in identifying provisions of the *Declaration* that can also be supported by state practice and *opinio juris*, with the possibility that some of its provisions do then reflect customary international law but with that established only with that additional evidence.

At present, Canadian courts are cautious as to any claim that the *Declaration* can be used in Canadian courtrooms in a straightforward way. But that does not mean it is irrelevant. The values it embodies are ones to which Canada aspires, and so will Canadian courts where its provisions are reasonable. Notably, in a recent case concerning statutory interpretation, the Federal Court stated as follows: "Indeed, while this instrument [the Declaration on the Rights of Indigenous Peoples] does not create substantive rights, the Court nonetheless favours an interpretation that will embody its values."[23] The *Declaration* is likely to have indirect and gradual effects on Canadian courts in so far as they treat it as an aspirational statement of Indigenous rights.

On consultation specifically, Canada's official representatives at the time of the vote saw elements of the *Declaration* as worrisome, significantly influencing Canada's decision to vote against it. Canada's reasons for opposition arose partly from the effects of the *Declaration* text in the context of the matters at stake relating to the duty to consult. The UN press release notes that John McNee, Canada's Ambassador to the United Nations, assured the General Assembly of Canada's ongoing strong support for Aboriginal rights, but indicated concerns with the *Declaration*:

> [S]ome of the provisions dealing with the concept of free, prior and informed consent were unduly restrictive, he said. Provisions in the Declaration said that States could not act on any legislative or administrative matter that might affect indigenous peoples without obtaining their consent. While Canada had a strong consultative pro-

22   *Ibid.*

23   *Simon v. Canada*, 2013 FC 1117 at para. 121.

cess, reinforced by the Courts as a matter of law, the establishment of complete veto power over legislative action for a particular group would be fundamentally incompatible with Canada's parliamentary system.[24]

The subsequent reading of the *Declaration*, which makes clear that it does not contain veto powers, but instead contains a spectrum analysis on consultation arguably having similarities to Canada's, has made it something Canada could endorse.[25] However, even as it has done so, the interpretation of the *Declaration* by the Special Rapporteur has arguably shifted. In mid-2013, the Special Rapporteur issued a report focused on Indigenous peoples and extractive resource industries.[26] This report, though still not adopting a veto power per se, did emphasize the rights of Indigenous peoples to withhold consent to resource developments on their traditional territories, something which begins to come remarkably close to a veto power.

Moreover, on the conclusion of a recent official visit to Canada in October 2013, the Special Rapporteur reemphasized this point in a press conference and specifically suggested that Canada's duty to consult doctrine fell short because it did not provide for the obtaining of free, prior, and informed consent to resource projects on traditional territories.[27] The Special Rapporteur will still write a formal report concerning the Canadian visit. But it does seem that, having endorsed the *Declaration* on one understanding of its meaning in relation to consultation, Canada may yet find that meaning to evolve over time. Although the *Declaration* will still not necessarily be binding international law on the point, Canada will be subjected to reports from the Special Rapporteur that seek to

---

24   UN Media Release, *supra* note 17.

25   This spectrum analysis is present in Annual Report of the United Nations Special Rapporteur on the Rights and Fundamental Freedoms of Indigenous People, U.N. Doc. A/HRC/12/34 (15 July 2009). I explain the implications and how this assisted Canada's endorsement in Newman, "Norms of Consultation with Indigenous Peoples," *supra* note 10.

26   Report of the Special Rapporteur on the Rights of Indigenous Peoples, James Anaya: Extractive Industries and Indigenous Peoples, UN Doc. A/HRC/24/41 (1 July 2013).

27   Roger Annis, "UN Rapporteur Wraps Up Visit with Stern Warning of Need for Action on Aboriginal Concerns," *Vancouver Observer* (16 October 2013).

hold it to account for a duty to consult doctrine that does not meet some aspirations within international law.

Canada's ongoing interaction with the *Declaration* on the duty to consult is part of an ongoing conversation in the international legal arena. At the moment, one would likely be right to see the Canadian duty to consult doctrine as part of the international law norm requiring some minimum degree of consultation with Indigenous peoples. Canada's doctrine is part of, and engaged with, international norms on relationships with Indigenous peoples. However, the evolution of international law in this area may have future impacts on the Canadian doctrine. To see that potential, we need to turn to some of the developing state practice outside Canada.

5.4 Australia and the Right to Negotiate

Given the trend toward transnational legal dialogue in various spheres — an enormous phenomenon in recent years — a possible source of impact on Canada's duty to consult is contained in other domestic legal orders with analogous doctrines, this impact being in two possible ways. First, in her judgement in *Haida Nation*, McLachlin C.J.C. refers to an early New Zealand document on consultation with the Maori,[28] illustrating the interest in comparative perspectives for their own sake. Second, notably, the legal systems of other states also amount to state practices for the purpose of identifying requirements of customary international law as well, speaking to another way in which they can exert longer-term influence on Canada.

One legal system of particular interest in this respect is that of Australia, which contrasts significantly with the somewhat general and even vague tone of international law in that it offers a rather detailed statutory framework of interest. Even a number of years on with the duty to consult doctrine, comparative considerations of the Canadian duty to consult doctrine have still not attracted much detailed consideration to date, despite the judicial references to New Zealand consultation documents discussed in *Haida Nation* — one notable exception being a 2005 paper by Daniel Guttman on *Australian and Canadian Approaches to Native Title* and another being some briefer passages within Paul McHugh's tremendous com-

---

28 *Haida Nation v. British Columbia (Minister of Forests)*, [2004] 3 S.C.R. 511, 2004 SCC 73 at para. 46. The reference is to *A Guide for Consultation with Maori* (Wellington: Ministry of Justice, 1997): www.justice.govt.nz/pubs/reports/1998/maori_consultation/index.html.

parative work on Aboriginal title doctrine.[29] The lack of discussion on the issue is somewhat surprising, given the level of interest by Australians in Canadian Aboriginal title cases such as *Delgamuukw,* and Canadian interest in the Australian decision in *Mabo and Others* v. *Queensland (No 2),*[30] a landmark case in which the term *terra nullius* — "land belonging to no-one" — was rendered null itself, making way for the recognition of a form of Native title.[31] This lack of attention to one another is unfortunate, for the Australian system has a particular salience for Canada that is not present in every attempt at comparative law in the Indigenous rights context.

Australia's consultation system has developed differently from the Canadian duty to consult doctrine, in that Australia's law in this area arises less from judicial decisions than from statutory norms. That being said, the development of the law was certainly prompted by judicial decisions, particularly the Australian High Court's decision in *Mabo.*[32] Following that decision, Australia chose to adopt a legislative framework on Aboriginal title in an attempt to clarify the area more rapidly than would have occurred through ongoing judicial development, and the government adopted the *Native Title Act, 1993,*[33] which entered into force on January 1, 1994. Following the next landmark decision of the High Court, *Wik Peoples* v. *Queensland,*[34] difficult debates ensued, and the government adopted major amendments to the statutory framework in 1998.[35]

A significant component of Australia's legislative framework is the "right to negotiate" arising in relation to "future acts," those acts done after 1 January 1994, that have effects on native title in Australia. The basic norm to this effect is found in subs. 25(2) of the *Native Title Act, 1993:* "Before

---

29   Daniel Guttman, "Australian and Canadian Approaches to Native Title Pre-Proof," [2005] Australian Indigenous Law Reporter 39: www.austlii.edu.au/au/journals/AILR/2005/39.html; Paul McHugh, *Aboriginal Title: The Modern Jurisprudence of Tribal Land Rights* (Oxford: Oxford University Press, 2011).

30   *Mabo and Others* v. *Queensland (No. 2),* [1992] HCA 23, (1992) 175 C.L.R. 1.

31   See Peter H. Russell, *Recognizing Aboriginal Title: The Mabo Case and Indigenous Resistance to English-Settler Colonialism* (Toronto: University of Toronto Press, 2005).

32   *Mabo and Others* v. *Queensland (No. 2), supra* note 30.

33   See Melissa Perry & Stephen Lloyd, *Australian Native Title Law* (Sydney: Lawbook, 2003).

34   *Wik Peoples* v. *The State of Queensland* (1996) 187 CLR 1 (Aust. H.C.).

35   *Native Title Amendment Act, 1998 (Aust. Cth.).*

the future act is done, the parties must negotiate with a view to reaching an agreement about the act." In relation to proposed government actions of certain types (especially mining-related grants and title-related grants to a third party), a compulsory negotiation process commences between the government, the third party beneficiary, and registered Native title holders and claimants.[36] There is a different procedure for future acts that have minimal effects, which can qualify for an expedited procedure, though there is a chance to object to something being fast-tracked in this manner.[37] There is a period in which negotiation is to occur, and, if that is unsuccessful, then matters go to the National Native Title Tribunal for adjudication on whether the action can go ahead and on what conditions.[38]

Pursuant to room in the Australian Commonwealth legislation for the development of state legislation, the Australian state of Queensland has chosen to develop its own right to negotiate framework in directions different than those chosen by the Commonwealth government, so as to offer greater clarity in the context of the state's mining industry.[39] The Queensland framework creates a two-tiered system, with low-impact exploration activities giving rise to a simpler regime of notification and consultation, and higher-impact mining activities giving rise to a larger right to negotiate.[40] The Queensland system is intended to be more applicant-driven, with the applicant for mining rights to which the high-impact system applies launching the process and assuming the greater responsibility for it.[41] It is also intended to refer stalled cases to a state-based Land and Resources Tribunal that will not have the backlog faced by the National Native Title Tribunal, with the hope of this speeding up the process.[42] The framework

---

36   *Native Title Act, 1993* (Aust. Cth.), ss. 26-30 provide much of the framework.

37   Section 29 of the *Act* provides for this.

38   *Native Title Act, 1993* (Aust. Cth.), ss. 35-36.

39   See *Native Title (Queensland) State Provisions Amendment Act (No 2), 1998* (Queensland); *Native Title State Provisions Act, 1999* (Queensland); and *Native Title Resolution Act, 2000* (Queensland). See also Kathrine Morgan-Wicks, "Balancing Native Title and Mining Interests: The Queensland Experience," in Christopher J. F. Boge (Ed.), *Justice for All? Native Title in the Australian Legal System* (Brisbane: Lawyers Books Publications, 2001), p. 65.

40   See Morgan-Wicks, *ibid.* at 68, 71-79.

41   *Ibid.* at 76, comparing s. 658 of the amended Queensland *Mineral Resources Act, 1989* with s. 30A of the national *Native Title Act*.

42   *Ibid.* at 74, 76, 84. An additional efficiency is gained by this tribunal having

is much more detailed than this description, but this hopefully gives some sense of it.

Other states that are significantly affected by the right to negotiate processes have similarly made decisions to develop particular policies. For example, the state of Western Australia has adopted a "whole-of-government" approach with strong parallels to similar initiatives at the federal government level in Canada. Within this approach, the Western Australia government has tried to reach some broader agreements, such as in the form of the final offer it made on the South West Settlement in July 2013.[43] There are many complex parallels and differences between issues in Australia and Canada, and there is meaningful scope for much more detailed comparative work on consultation and related issues in these two countries.

Within a framework developing a procedural right paralleling the duty to consult through statute, Australia's governments have become engaged in the development of detailed procedures, particularly to try to balance the complex needs of resource extraction industries with the rights of Australia's Indigenous communities. Similarly detailed processes cannot arise as readily, or as systematically, from the development of the Canadian duty to consult through case law. That said, the statutory option is not obviously present in the Canadian context. Particularly in relation to resource industries, where provinces have strongly taken jurisdictional authority since the 1982 constitutional amendments, the federal government would face a difficult division of powers barrier in enacting legislation to clarify the duty to consult.[44] At the same time, the overriding federal jurisdiction in relation to Aboriginal communities, particularly Aboriginal title or rights,[45] would render it difficult for a province to enact legislation to clarify the duty to consult through statutory norms. Though there might be ways around this division-of-powers Catch-22 — British Columbia believed at one point

---

simultaneous jurisdiction in relation to the right to negotiate issues along with cultural heritage objects issues. Challenges obviously arise if this Tribunal becomes backlogged.

43   For a summary, see http://www.dpc.wa.gov.au/lantu/MediaPublications/Documents/The%20South%20West%20Settlement-A-Summary-July-2013-Final.pdf.

44   The *Constitution Act, 1867* had added to its division of powers provisions the provincial resources jurisdiction in s. 92A.

45   *Ibid.* s. 91(24) grants jurisdiction to the federal government over legislation related to "Indians, and Lands reserved for the Indians."

that it had found some (see discussion in Chapter 4) — the more probable course will be ongoing elaboration of provincial policy rather than legislation, and the establishment of practices at the interaction points of government, corporate, and Aboriginal policies.

The Australian example does illustrate how some of the same issues that have been challenging in Canada have been subject to different legislative consideration. The issue of the role of applicant corporations seeking to explore or develop particular resources would have been a matter for different consideration under the Queensland framework than under the national framework. Those developing Canadian policies and practice are well advised to be carefully attuned to the needs in particular areas and sectors for larger governmental or industry roles.

Australia's system has a fundamental route around its right-to-negotiate system with the possibility of negotiated "Indigenous Land Use Agreements."[46] Such agreements, once they make it through a registration process, bind all Native title holders in a certain area.[47] If mining companies can identify correctly the relevant Native title parties and develop friendly relationships that foster win-win solutions, they may effectively negotiate around the right-to-negotiate system. The Australian experience has actually featured a massive use of these agreements, which have generated significant academic writing in Australia.[48]

This dimension of Australia's framework aptly illustrates how the procedural rights created within one system can establish bargaining strength that communities may try to "trade" for substantive outcomes within other rights systems — namely, those concerned with substantive rights connected with Native title or compensatory frameworks. Thus, there have been attempts by Native representatives in Australia to "trade" procedural

---

46   *Native Title Act, 1993* (Aust. Cth.), s. 24. See also the discussion in Russell, *supra* note 31 at 371-75.

47   *Ibid.* ss. 24BB, 24CB, 24DB.

48   See especially Ciaran O'Faircheallaigh, "Use and Management of Revenues from Indigenous-Mining Company Agreements: Theoretical Perspectives" (July 2011) ATNS Working Paper No 1: http://www.atns.net.au/website/workingpapers.asp; Ciaran O'Faircheallaigh, "Aboriginal – Mining Company Contractual Agreements in Australia and Canada: Implications for Political Autonomy and Community Development" (2010) 30 Canadian Journal of Development Studies 69-86; Ciaran O'Faircheallaigh, "Negotiating Protection of the Sacred? Aboriginal-Mining Company Agreements in Australia" (2008) 39 Development and Change 25-51.

negotiation rights for compensation related to the value of minerals at issue, such as through obtaining royalty rights.[49] This mode of compensation does not entirely match the valuation methods within the Australian legislation, which is concerned more with the effect on the Indigenous community as the background legal condition — although allowing for negotiation of profit-sharing in some circumstances[50] — but it may nonetheless become a practicable mode for those paying compensation in the context of certain resource developments, partly because it is a gradual mode of payment occurring alongside future output.[51] However, gradual payments also contain the danger of future disputes for resource companies.[52] Moreover, any transition to such compensation systems may exert pressures on other contexts, even internationally, as networks of advocates become aware of solutions developed in other contexts. Canadian resource companies faced with such possibilities will find themselves in complex and difficult situations, particularly if a company can gain a competitive advantage by launching a compensation system beyond the legal rights discussed in Chapter 3, but in doing so possibly alter the compensation frameworks for others in the future.

Aboriginal communities, of course, have every reason to press for such possibilities, particularly as they become more aware of elements of the Australian experience. As discussed in Chapter 4, many Aboriginal communities have been pushing for compensatory frameworks in the context of the duty to consult. Informed in part by comparative legal experience, the ultimate shape of the doctrine in action will depend on ongoing negotiations.

---

49   See K.D. MacDonald, "Commercial Implications of Native Title for Mining and Resources," in Bryan Horrigan & Simon Young (Eds.), *Commercial Implications of Native Title* (Sydney: Federation Press, 1997) at 122-23.

50   See *Native Title Act, 1993*, *supra* note 36 at ss. 33, 38(2). These sections imply that profit-sharing can be developed in negotiated resolutions but cannot be imposed through arbitration.

51   MacDonald, *supra* note 49 at 123.

52   *Ibid.*

5.5 Consultation Norms in Latin America

The decision of the Inter-American Court of Human Rights in *Saray-aku* v. *Ecuador*,[53] in which that Court indicated its view that consultation with Indigenous peoples is now a general principle of international law, also illustrates a broader pattern of decision-making on consultation in Latin America. The case concerned petroleum development in a part of the Amazon where the Sarayaku Indigenous peoples had asserted claims. Many of the Court's determinations that Ecuador had breached Sarayaku Indigenous rights were based on ILO Convention No. 169, to which Ecuador is a party, as are many Latin American states.

At the same time, consultation is also becoming part of the domestic law of various Latin American states in sometimes interesting ways. Aside from the Sarayaku decision at the Inter-American Court, Ecuador had had a previous case based simply on domestic law in which its Constitutional Court had ruled that a lack of consultation was an element of rights violations against the Shuar Indigenous people.[54]

In other developments, Peru became the first Latin American state to develop legislation on consultation in August 2011, with the adoption of the *Ley de Derecho a la Consulta Previa a los Pueblos Indígenas u Originarios Reconocido*.[55] This law follows on a longer period of developing case law on consultation in the Peruvian courts, which is the subject of ongoing study by a legal scholar, Alvaro Cordova.[56] But the legislation provides more detailed law on the matter, including through more recently adopted regulations.[57]

Bolivia has actually entrenched a number of different provisions on con-

---

53 *Kichwa Indigenous People of Sarayaku* v. *Ecuador, supra* note 7.

54 *Federacion Independiente del Pueblo Shuar del Ecuador* v. *Compania ARCO Orient Inc.* (Sentencia de 16, marzo de 2000).

55 Ley No 29785 (7 September 2011) (Peru), available online with associate regulations: http://consultaprevia.cultura.gob.pe/compendio-normativo.pdf.

56 He presented an initial version of this study as "The Right of Indigenous Self-Determination and Right to Consultation in the Peruvian Constitutional Tribunal Jurisprudence (2005-2011)" (LL.M. thesis, University of Victoria, 2013), and it is to be hoped that he publishes from this and his ongoing doctoral work at McGill.

57 Regulations were promulgated in April 2012 that create procedures for the *Ley de Consulta Previa*.

sultation in its Constitution.[58] Ecuador's 2008 Constitution similarly contains an article elaborating consultation requirements.[59] And these various instances are just some examples. Latin American states have moved significantly in recent years toward greater recognition of obligations of consultation with Indigenous peoples. Many such recognitions are in the context of states that owe specific treaty obligations because of ILO Convention No. 169. But they are nonetheless part of developing international practice in general terms.

It perhaps bears noting that Canadian companies operating abroad have in some instances found themselves to be affected by this developing law. To mention just one of a number of possible examples, there were moves toward the suspension of Goldcorp's Marlin Mine in Guatemala in 2010 and 2011, as a provisional measure arising from lack of consultation with Indigenous communities concerning the impact on them. Although the issues appear to have been resolved on an interim basis, the case stands as an example of how failure to consider developing practices on consultation abroad may well affect Canadian companies' international operations.

5.6 Other State Practice on Consultation

Consultation is no longer a niche topic. It fundamentally affects various areas of law on resource development. Thus, it should come as no surprise that it features as an important legal consideration within a legal text on mining. A recent text describes consultation-like requirements in the

---

58 *Constitution of Bolivia* (2009), ss. 30(15), 30(16), 352.

59 *Constitution of the Republic of Ecuador* (2008), art. 57.7 (which states in a typical English translation) that Indigenous communes, communities, peoples and nations are recognized and guaranteed, in conformity with the Constitution and human rights agreements, conventions, declarations and other international instruments, the following collective rights: [...]"To free prior informed consultation, within a reasonable period of time, on the plans and programs for prospecting, producing and marketing nonrenewable resources located on their lands and which could have an environmental or cultural impact on them; to participate in the profits earned from these projects and to receive compensation for social, cultural and environmental damages caused to them. The consultation that must be conducted by the competent authorities shall be mandatory and in due time. If consent of the consulted community is not obtained, steps provided for by the Constitution and the law shall be taken."

domestic law of Argentina, Australia, Brazil, Canada, Colombia, Finland, Mexico, Namibia, and Venezuela, with these states being the bulk of major mining states with agreed, defined Indigenous populations.[60]

The reality is that consultation is indeed developing as a norm concerning relations with Indigenous peoples across a wide variety of states. Frameworks for Indigenous consultation, and indeed for Indigenous economic participation in development, exist across a wide variety of states, far beyond what this book can survey in the context of one chapter on developing international law on consultation. I would refer readers, though, to other writing that does survey this developing practice. In a co-authored article on Arctic energy development and practices of consultation and economic participation, I have described developments in this regard being present in every Arctic state with Indigenous peoples.[61] The Inter-American Court lists some developments in a wide variety of states in the context of its reasoning toward the conclusion that consultation is a general principle of international law.[62] And the International Law Association released a major report in 2012 on the rights of Indigenous peoples in which it surveyed practice in a wide variety of states in an attempt to ascertain what practices might be developing into customary norms.[63]

It bears noting that I have not here focused on the United States. Comparisons between Canada and the United States in the Indigenous rights area are more complex than many might first assume, as the historical interaction of these two states with their Indigenous peoples has differed significantly. The United States has some much longer-standing practices of tribal self-government and of economic participation, particularly by Alaskan tribes in resource revenues, than is the case in Canada, but both also mean very different things in Canada. Those larger comparisons are more properly pursued elsewhere. However, it is possible to note briefly that even this nearest neighbour of Canada is similarly developing consultation policies.

On November 5th 2009, US President Obama signed and distributed

---

60   Stewart Sutcliffe (Ed.), *Mining Law: Jurisdictional Comparisons*, 1ˢᵗ ed. *(U.K.: Sweet & Maxwell, 2012)* at 126, 145, 158, 170-71, 184, 201, 225, 248, 314.

61   See Dwight Newman, Michelle Biddulph, & Lorelle Binnion, "Arctic Energy Development and Best Practices on Consultation with Indigenous Peoples" (2014) 32: 2 Boston U. Int'l L.J. (forthcoming).

62   *Kichwa Indigenous People of Sarayaku* v. *Ecuador, supra* note 7 at para. 164.

63   International Law Association, Resolution No. 5/2012, Appendix.

a memorandum on tribal consultation policies to pertinent government departments.[64] This memorandum emphasizes the unique relationship between the United States government and Indigenous communities and emphasizes the role of consultation with tribes affected by government action. There have also been more specific consultation policies announced by various government agencies, including the EPA,[65] the Department of the Interior,[66] the Department of Energy,[67] and others.[68] All of these policies look to whether a contemplated action will have a "substantial direct effect on an Indian Tribe."[69] And, in December 2011, the United States became the last of the four states that initially voted against the *Declaration on the Rights of Indigenous Peoples* to issue a qualified statement supporting the *Declaration*, further signalling the extent to which an international consensus is developing on a number of Indigenous rights issues.

5.7 Emerging International Law Norms of Consultation

The International Law Association, at its 2012 Sofia meeting, adopted a resolution to adopt a report in which it had attempted to examine which rights of Indigenous peoples had and had not become customary international law.[70] In that report, on the specific question of consultation, the International Law Association articulated as follows:

In sum, international practice concerning this delicate issue [con-

---

64   Office of the Press Secretary, Executive Office of the President, Memorandum for the Heads of Executive Departments and Agencies: Tribal Consultation (2009).

65   United States Environmental Protection Agency, EPA Policy on Consultation and Coordination with Indian Tribes (2011) at 3.

66   United States Department of the Interior, Department of the Interior Policy on Consultation with Indian Tribes (2011).

67   United States Department of Energy, American Indian & Alaskan Native Tribal Government Policy (2009).

68   See White House Indian Affairs Executive Working Group, List of Federal Tribal Consultation Statutes, Orders, Regulations, Rules, Policies, Manuals, Protocols, and Guidance (2009) at 5-16 (a list of all the relevant departmental rules and policies, including links to the full-text of each of those policies).

69   See, e.g., Department of the Interior Policy, *supra* note 66 at 3 (other policies have similar wording).

70   International Law Association, Resolution No. 5/2012, Appendix.

sultation and FPIC] is clearly heterogeneous; this circumstance confirms that the right contemplated by Article 19 UNDRIP does not imply the existence of a right to veto – *in general terms* – with respect to *every kind of measure* that may affect indigenous peoples.[71]

This statement aptly recognizes that there is significant developing practice but that it varies significantly from one state to the next. However, saying that much does not call into question a statement of James Anaya, writing in his scholarly capacity, that "[t]he provisions of Convention No. 169 and the draft declarations . . . represent a consensus that extends well beyond states that have ratified Convention No. 169 or the authorized experts that developed the drafts."[72] Anaya made other points specifically in relation to provisions on participation and consultation, noting, for instance, that the World Bank had taken on these concerns in its operational policies, and concluding, from states' comments, that "[i]t is evident that there exists a broad acceptance of minimum requirements of consultation among states and others participating in the discussions on these drafts, even while certain disagreement persists about the particular wording that should make its way into the final declarations."[73] One could interpret this consensus as continuing through the formulation of the final *Declaration*, which obviously gained the assent of more states.

There has not developed an international practice of states having to obtain free, prior, and informed consent for all activities affecting Indigenous peoples, although concepts of free, prior, and informed consent are part

---

71   *Ibid.* at 6.

72   Anaya, *Indigenous Peoples in International Law, supra* note 1.

73   *Ibid.*, 155. The texts of the *Draft Declaration* of 1994 and the final *Declaration* of 2007 refer in their later forms to a requirement of free, prior, and informed consent for legislative and administrative decisions that affect Aboriginal communities, differing from the wording in Article 6 of the ILO Convention, which had referred to efforts to attain agreement. This represents a certain hardening of the wording of the consultation requirements. The texts of the *Draft* and final *Declaration* on consultation in the context of resource development similarly refer to free, prior, and informed consent before resource development can proceed, whereas Article 15(2) of the ILO Convention had referred to efforts to attain agreement, to participation where possible in the economic activity, and to compensation for damage resulting, again reflecting a hardening of the wording.

of ongoing international conversations. Rather, the international law on consultation has arguably developed toward a spectrum analysis, in which free, prior, and informed consent potentially applies as a standard only to activities with a particularly severe impact on Indigenous peoples.

Canada's duty to consult doctrines are at the heart of an ongoing development of state practice within the international order, both contributing to and engaged with the norms developing within the international order in relation to Indigenous peoples. Canadian Aboriginal leaders have sought to link the duty to consult doctrine to this larger framework,[74] as have some government documents.[75] The ongoing development of the international regime on these matters surely includes some expectation of consultation with Indigenous peoples. However, thus far, a full reading of international law likely does not see this expectation as encompassing free, prior, and informed consent as often as some claim it applies. But the law continues to evolve.

5.8 Staying Ahead of the Regulatory Curve

Various parties and stakeholders that are contemplating longer-term strategic action need to consider not just what the law is today but what the law will be in ten years' time or even decades down the road. Certain mining developments, as one example, will involve the construction of facilities with planned multi-decade lifespans. Those considering such developments need to consider the potential effects of future legal developments as well as the present law. In other words, there is always an inherent challenge of staying ahead of the regulatory curve so as to carry out developments in ways that will not be rendered futile some years along in the process.

Some will think of staying ahead of the regulatory curve in another manner as well. Businesses that have practices that do not require major changes in light of likely legal developments may gain a competitive advan-

---

74   See Assembly of First Nations Resolution No. 22 (2008): www.afn.ca/article. asp?id=4285. See also British Columbia Assembly of First Nations 4th Annual Regional Chiefs' Special Assembly Res. No. 17/2008 (Feb. 2008): www.bcafn. ca/index.php?option=com_docman&task=doc_view&gid=371.

75   One example appears in Canada's Statement on Examples of Applications of the Principle of Free, Prior, and Informed Consent (FPIC) at the National and International Levels (Geneva, July 2005): www.ainc-inac.gc.ca/ap/ia/stmt/ unp/05/pop/anx-eng.asp.

tage from these practices. Although the use of future-ready practices does not eliminate the need to keep close tabs on ongoing regulatory development, it may allow for greater business stability through challenging times when the development of new practices will generate significant costs if carried out only in response to regulatory developments.

Those thinking ahead in some manner to where the law will be in future need to consider not only Canadian constitutional developments but the ongoing development of international law as well. In this sense, to understand the duty to consult, one needs to understand not only the specificities of Canadian constitutional law but the broader international law treatment of Indigenous peoples.

5.9 Conclusion

Whatever Canada does in terms of the duty to consult, it does not act in "splendid isolation." Our relationship with Indigenous peoples exists in the context of a set of developing international norms. Along with norms developed in specific comparative contexts, our approach becomes an instance of state practice in the ongoing development of these norms. Although some claims concerning the contents of international law are less certain than they might first appear, it is nonetheless the case that international law may affect the future development of Canada's duty to consult doctrine. Our doctrine may also be affected by comparative doctrine in other countries that are facing similar questions. The duty to consult doctrine is not static, but contains potential for ongoing growth in light of international developments.

6

Understanding the Duty to Consult

THIS BOOK, IN BOTH ITS FIRST EDITION IN 2009 and this revised edition of 2014, has attempted a number of things. Some of these have been focused on simpler understandings of the duty to consult, but the hope is also to reach some deeper understandings as well. Chapter 1 introduced the modern duty to consult doctrine and set out a number of possible theoretical approaches to understanding it. Chapters 2 and 3 set out a number of doctrinal parameters on the doctrine as it has developed, with Chapter 2 dealing with legal parameters such as the triggering conditions and who is involved in a consultation, and Chapter 3 dealing with the content of a consultation. Chapter 4 showed the ways in which the lower court case law behind Chapters 2 and 3 has left room for the development of much more policy and practice by governments, Aboriginal communities, and industry stakeholders that is seeing the doctrine develop in further ways. Chapter 5 showed some possible future influences on the doctrine so far as it is rooted in, engaged in, and subject to influence from transnational components in international and comparative law, and these latter parts especially have grown in the context of changes over recent years.

In some senses, the aim of understanding the duty to consult would now arguably call for assessing which of the theoretical models mentioned in Chapter 1 has the best "fit" with the doctrine as developed through lower court judgements discussed in Chapters 2 and 3, with the "law in action" as developed in Chapter 4, and with the evolving possibilities of international and comparative law in Chapter 5. In other senses, this might look like a problematic task, for the nature of what has gone on in the context of the duty to consult features many moves arising from power relations or from what appears to work in particular circumstances. Ultimately, as well, the duty may not be explained by one simple underlying principle but rather embody a set of considerations.

In terms of the theoretical approaches of Chapter 1, the duty to consult is about a relationship between the Crown and Aboriginal peoples, and might be thought of in terms of honourable relationships, but the duty to consult is about more than this. It is about the ways in which government stakeholders, Aboriginal stakeholders, corporate stakeholders, and ultimately all Canadians can co-exist in ways living out honour while allowing for the development of new futures. To say this much is to suggest that the duty to consult can, and must, serve multiple purposes at the same time. Indeed, the Supreme Court of Canada, in its *Rio Tinto* decision, has embraced such a vision:

> The duty to consult is grounded in the honour of the Crown. It is a corollary of the Crown's obligation to achieve the just settlement of Aboriginal claims through the treaty process. While the treaty claims process is ongoing, there is an implied duty to consult with the Aboriginal claimants on matters that may adversely affect their treaty and Aboriginal rights, and to accommodate those interests in the spirit of reconciliation: *Haida Nation*, at para. 20.
>
> [...]
>
> As the post-*Haida Nation* case law confirms, consultation is "[c]oncerned with an ethic of ongoing relationships" and seeks to further an ongoing process of reconciliation by articulating a preference for remedies "that promote ongoing negotiations": D. G. Newman, *The Duty to Consult: New Relationships with Aboriginal Peoples* (2009), at p. 21.[1]

These paragraphs reference the role of the duty to consult in maintaining Crown honour, in pursuing the just settlement of Aboriginal claims, and in fostering ongoing relationships and reconciliation. It must thus serve multiple functions.

To describe the duty to consult in terms of the honour of the Crown is to describe something about it but to do so in a perhaps too focused way. The duty to consult is about fostering negotiation processes and ensuring that actions that take place in advance of concluded negotiations or judicial de-

---

1   *Rio Tinto Alcan Inc.* v. *Carrier Sekani Tribal Council*, 2010 SCC 43, [2010] 2 SCR 650, at paras. 32, 38.

cisions will not be to the unreasonable detriment of Aboriginal stakeholders. There are contexts where this element is central to the duty to consult,
but they can involve a defensive conception of it where there are also much
richer ways in which it is developing. The duty to consult is also about an
economically efficient means of addressing issues, rather than using the set
of injunctions that the full array of Aboriginal rights and title claims could
generate. But it is far from solely an economic doctrine. The duty to consult
may in some instances be a vehicle of reconciliation or the generation of
new norms that further it, but the doctrinal limits on it also make it a limited vehicle for pursuing those aims in some circumstances.

There has arguably been in many contexts a deeply pragmatic sense to
the way in which the duty to consult has developed. Much of the doctrine
and policy has been related to what will work. At the same time, many
doctrinal decisions indicate a deep rootedness in principle, with the underlying principles of the duty to consult helping to determine previously unresolved questions on the doctrine. Realizing some of the pragmatism of
the duty to consult must raise questions about to what extent it should be
thought of in terms of the honour of the Crown. The ongoing development
of a Supreme Court of Canada jurisprudence focused heavily on the honour of the Crown in defining Crown obligations opens some challenging
questions. In the *Manitoba Métis Federation* case,[2] the Court develops a
broader idea of the honour of the Crown as a source of Crown obligations,
with solemn obligations of diligent fulfillment of Crown commitments
seemingly developing as a further offshoot of the honour principle alongside the duty to consult. The dissenting justices pertinently point to the
challenges of identifying all the Crown obligations that may arise. There
are presently significant questions on just what the full scope of the honour
of the Crown concept is going to be, and some of the scope of this set of
obligations is implicitly driven by the expansion of the duty to consult. So
far as the duty to consult is explained in terms of the honour of the Crown,
the honour of the Crown must be expansive enough to explain what has
become a widening duty to consult doctrine. In turn, there may be un-
predictable ramifications via other doctrines that may then be rooted in a
substantially broadened honour of the Crown.

At the same time, focusing on the honour of the Crown has a potentially
limiting dimension. A focus on the honour of the Crown is in some degree

---

2   *Manitoba Métis Federation Inc. v. Canada (Attorney General)*, 2013 SCC 14.

of competition with an account of the duty to consult that sees it as aligned with a set of international developments on consultation with Indigenous peoples. The honour of the Crown is a principle uniquely fitting a constitutional monarchy like Canada but not the broader spectrum of states in the international arena. Any overemphasis on the honour of the Crown would have some effects of distancing Canadian duty to consult doctrine from potential effects of ongoing international developments. That said, there are possible arguments that this distancing is a good thing that enables Canadian law to respond more specifically to Canadian circumstances. The possibility that international law is moving toward a duty to consult on legislative action does not necessarily mean that the creation of such a constitutional duty in the Canadian context would be a wise move. As discussed in Chapter 3, such a duty would alter fundamental features of Canadian democratic processes, and it would also make policy changes for the benefit of Aboriginal communities more challenging in the face of internal differences within the broader Aboriginal community. It may be that a more localized theoretical foundation has its advantages as well.

That said, recognizing the pragmatic ways the duty to consult has functioned as a judicial innovation allowing responses to uncertainty on the scope of different Aboriginal and treaty rights casts a different light on the doctrine where anyone engaged with the doctrine should be fundamentally concerned with its effects, more so than with any neat theoretical underpinnings. The effects of the duty to consult doctrine are enormously far-reaching, quite possibly far more so than the judges who adopted the modern form of the doctrine ever foresaw or are fully contemplating today.

One interesting dimension of the duty to consult doctrine is its ability to crowd out other Aboriginal rights litigation. Although the Supreme Court of Canada has recently heard the *Roger William* or *Tsilhqot'in Nation case*,[3] as a case on the substantive scope of Aboriginal title, cases on substantive points of Aboriginal or treaty rights have in some ways become the exception. There are many incentives to put arguments based on the duty to consult, and to litigate on the duty to consult if necessary, rather than to seek a judgement that makes a final determination on an Aboriginal or treaty right. This dynamic arises because what is available via interim means under the duty to consult is significantly better than the result if an Aboriginal community litigates on a substantive point and loses. The

---

3   *William* v. *British Columbia*, 2012 BCCA 285, leave to appeal to Supreme Court of Canada granted 24 January 2013 and hearing held 7 November 2013.

recent example of the *Hirsekorn* case in southern Alberta illustrates this point.[4] In this case, the Métis community of Alberta developed its own harvesting plans to assert their rights after they considered the government plans for Métis hunting too restrictive. The case functioned as a test case, with Hirsekorn hunting in the Cypress Hills in accordance with the plans. However, Hirsekorn lost in the Alberta Court of Appeal and was denied leave to appeal to the Supreme Court of Canada. The result is effectively a definitive denial of Métis hunting rights rather than a partial set of rights that could have been obtained through maintaining uncertainty and then seeking accommodation based on the duty to consult.

A similar dynamic is arguably at play in the context of many claims related to resource revenue sharing. The assertion of Aboriginal and treaty rights related to resources ends up encouraging governments, in the context of the duty to consult framework, to be more open to resource revenue sharing than ever before — although some governments have remained very clear on the ideal of natural resources being for the benefit of the entire population of their respective provinces. In some provinces, Aboriginal communities argue that some of the numbered treaties, according to their oral traditions, actually ceded ownership of land only "to the depth of a plough."[5] At the same time, there are meaningful arguments in the treaty texts and history against that interpretation. Any litigation of the point would potentially have dramatic consequences one way or the other if the courts reached a definitive conclusion on the point. In some ways, both Aboriginal communities and governments are happy to proceed in some degree of uncertainty and simply to find arrangements that hopefully work from a policy standpoint. The duty to consult can facilitate the creative use of ambiguity, although the flip side is that it may also help encourage parties to perpetuate uncertainty that imposes significant costs in its own right.

Given its new dominance in the Aboriginal law field, more detailed features of how the duty to consult operates also have very significant effects that are not always contemplated. As discussed in this book, the focus of the duty to consult has remained thus far on consultation with the rights-bearing community. Yet, within some Aboriginal community contexts, in-

---

4   *R. v. Hirsekorn*, 2013 ABCA 242, leave to appeal to Supreme Court of Canada denied 24 January 2014.

5   For discussion, see Dwight Newman, *Natural Resource Jurisdiction in Canada* (Toronto: LexisNexis, 2013).

dividual Aboriginal community members would prefer to have consultation with the individuals whose interests are most affected by a particular project or decision. For example, there will be many kinds of developments that have the potential to impact upon the use of trap lines and other traditional resource uses. Individual trappers or traditional resource users who make use of a particular area will be those impacted by the development, more tangibly than the overall rights-bearing community. Individual trappers or traditional resource users may actually want compensation for the effect on their own established rights, which verge on a sort of property right. An ongoing focus on consultation with a rights-bearing community makes a political choice of sorts between different interests in Aboriginal communities. These questions are often totally veiled, and they remain implicit even in a case where they started to emerge, the *Behn* v. *Moulton Contracting* case.[6] But that case signals that these questions may well end up again before the courts. The courts will need to contemplate carefully their stance on to what degree the duty to consult doctrine should operate in a way that specifically reinforces one side of a broader discussion with Aboriginal communities.

The duty to consult doctrine and the ways in which it is implemented also have other effects on Aboriginal communities, such as in possible effects on power structures within communities. In communities where the duty to consult has been leveraged into impact benefit agreements or similar arrangements, there will commonly be a business arm of the community that gains significant benefits and power as a result. This business arm will typically be a different structure apart from any *Indian Act* governance structure or traditional governance structure. The power accumulated within the business arm of the community introduces an additional force within community governance, with some of the developments associated with the duty to consult thus having complex political, sociological, and cultural effects on Aboriginal communities.

The economic gains from the duty to consult are very real for some Aboriginal communities. Where the duty to consult doctrine has helped create pressures for the development of impact benefit agreements, those IBAs have in some Aboriginal communities led to the injection of literally hundreds of millions of dollars of resource revenue or business revenue associated with service provision to resource industries. One issue that will

---

6   *Behn* v. *Moulton Contracting Ltd.*, 2013 SCC 26.

become more complicated over time is a potential growing inequality as between different Aboriginal communities, arising from a combination of a different resource potential available to different communities and different capacities to leverage the duty to consult. Growing inequality as between different Aboriginal communities over time will actually create complex legal and political dynamics, with different Aboriginal communities likely to adopt increasingly different stances on a range of policy issues.

In terms of the economic effects of the duty to consult, however, we also must not forget the significant possible costs of the duty if it becomes something that interferes in unreasonable ways with lawful development activities. Many Aboriginal communities are highly supportive of economic development and seek to participate in it in the ways the duty to consult can help facilitate, while also benefiting from the ways in which the duty to consult can protect core cultural and spiritual interests that are not for sale. However, in the instance of a development project that affects more than one Aboriginal community, complex dynamics can arise where some communities either simply refuse to be supportive or are trying to leverage significant benefits for themselves, at the expense of other communities. More broadly, if law and policy do not ensure that the duty to consult works efficiently, the delays occasioned by the duty to consult will sometimes be so prolonged as to render projects no longer economically feasible that would have generated significant benefits for Aboriginal communities themselves. The legal uncertainties around the duty to consult also risk scaring away some investors.

These effects do not in any way imply that there should not be respect for Aboriginal and treaty rights. But they do say that it is important that courts and policy-makers continue to ensure that the duty to consult fulfills its purposes as a procedure but does not become an effective veto power, which it is not meant to be. Even in the international arena, something akin to a veto power arises only from the most dramatic effects on a community's core interests. In other circumstances, consultation should not become a pretext to block lawful activities. Responsible resource development can benefit non-Aboriginal and Aboriginal communities alike. Courts and policy-makers dealing with the duty to consult need to consider carefully all of the complex dynamics associated with it and ensure they continue developing it in forms that work well for all.

The duty to consult is a complex doctrine that embodies a number of related aims and aspirations that give rise to various principles related to it. It has room to grow in these principled ways and in localized ways that work. As within any area of the common law, its ongoing development will continue to take time. We may thus foresee that there will be ongoing development in the duty to consult, and this is an exciting, enriching element of a diverse Canada.

Index

adverse effect element of duty to consult as trigger 38–39, 42, 46–52, 90
   government action not confined to immediate impact 55, 104
   severity of 46–47, 96–97, 60

Affolder, Natasha 134

Ahousaht First Nation v. *Canada (Minister of Finance)* 45, 59n81, 70, 89–90, 95n31

Alberta Clipper Pipeline 75–76, 137n75

Alberta: consultation policies 121n20, 122, 123
   Metis excluded in 122

Anaya, James 163

Arnot, David 28

Assembly of First Nations (AFN) 128
   Resolution No.22 164n74

Athabasca Chipewyan First Nation v. *Alberta (Minister of Energy)* 52n55

Australia
   compared to Canadian system 125, 138, 153–54, 156
   compulsory negotiation process 155
   Indigenous Land Use Agreements 157
   Queensland version of right to negotiate 155, 157
   "Right to Negotiate" 153–58
   and UN *Declaration* 150
   whole-of-government approach 156

Barnes, J. 101–02

Beaver Lake Cree Nation 111

Beckman v. *Little Salmon/ Carmacks First Nation* (*Little Salmon*) 10, 21
   on modern treaties 43, 81–82
   notice 99n42

Behn v. *Moulton Contracting* 10
   duty owed to individuals 21–22, 65, 171

Bill 70 (Quebec) 127n40

Bill C-45 62–63

Bolivia: on consultation 159–60

breaches of duty to consult 44, 70, 98
   in *Haida Nation* 17–18, 48–49
   historic 19, 49, 51–52, 102–03
   in *Lefthand* 47
   remedies 26, 33, 77–78, 167